DEDICATION

This book is dedicated to Mark, Nolan, and Bridget.
Thank you for loving me for me.

NOSH

What My Sabbatical Taught Me About Connection, One Lunch at a Time

Heather L. Cleary

Nosh: What My Sabbatical Taught Me About Connection, One Lunch at a Time

ISBN: 979-8-9992030-3-8

Book Design by Transcendent Publishing | TranscendentPublishing.com
Edited by Mary Rembert
Author Photo by Mike Tabolsky

Printed in the United States of America.

"Meals make the society, hold the fabric together in lots of ways that were charming and interesting and intoxicating to me. The perfect meal, or the best meals, occur in a context that frequently has very little to do with the food itself."

—Anthony Bourdain

TABLE OF CONTENTS

INTRODUCTION

My career path has been one of starts, stops, dramatic swings, and slight directional realignments. By 2018, I had worked for Starbucks® Coffee Company for twelve years.

There were two very notable and unique benefits I enjoyed at Starbucks. First, each week, I received a free pound of coffee (known as "markout") made available to Starbucks Partners (employees) from day one. Second, a Partner became eligible for an unpaid sabbatical after ten consecutive years of working, cleverly named a "Coffee Break."

Around 2016, I began to plan for my Coffee Break. Several considerations supported the idea. First, my oldest child, near the end of high school, would be starting the college admissions process as his next step.

Second, my youngest, only two years behind her brother in high school, would also start her process of searching for colleges.

Third, I itched to travel to research a music book I wanted to write.

Fourth, I fixated on the idea of uninterrupted time with my family as a big attraction.

Finally, my energy had waned because my burnout increased to a critical level. Self-care became a large factor.

In the months leading up to my Coffee Break, I inherently knew there would be a point where I would experience isolation. Abruptly, my weekday life would cease, as I would no longer work in a corporate office building with its bodies coming and going. I was used to being a part of a corporate community of roughly 5,000 people in one building. Overnight, the chaos, noise, and proximity of others would be instantaneously removed from my life.

Although I have a husband and two teenage children, I knew the normalcy of my sabbatical days would typically consist of me and my two cats, Cora and Callie. I ascertained that there would be a major adjustment, not too dissimilar from when an athlete retires from a sport. The quiet would be daunting.

Even with an abundance of plans, I suspected the "now what?" question would surface. I was wise enough to know that I needed to have a plan to combat the potential loneliness and isolation. The ability to say hellos or pleasantries to numerous coworkers on the stairs, in meeting rooms, and at lunch would vanish for a period of time.

There are two things in this world that I absolutely cherish: routine and challenges. How could I create a routine in a life that was now flush with time? How could I do something that continuously challenged me for a year?

That was when an idea formed. What is the one way I could engage in the most basic, yet essential, of human connections? Lunches! The goal: to have lunch with a different person each week. Fifty-two lunches, with fifty-two different people. Simply put, lunch with the normal expectations that occur during a meal in a restaurant. No hard-and-fast rules and no interview questions. This idea fulfilled the notion of a routine and provided a good challenge.

A plan began to formulate in my head on how to do this. Who to include? Did I know fifty-two people? That last question was quickly answered when I started creating a list of family, friends, coworkers, acquaintances, and so on. Of course, I knew fifty-two different people. The bigger challenge was whether I had fifty-two different outfits to wear.

The concept was not complicated: the invitee for that specific week would select their preferred restaurant on the designated day, time, and duration. With that in mind, I would be respectful of time during a workday. Or, in the case of those not working, if more than an hour lunchtime was allotted, I would gladly indulge that too.

No questions, no interviews, no exposés. My only request was for permission to highlight the lunch in a blog post. In the blog, I would use only first names and their photo if they consented. For many of the lunches, if we discussed a topic that might be difficult, sensitive, or troubling, I asked for permission to include that in my blog post.

I intended to keep my blog entries to approximately 1,000 words. I did not want to drivel on unnecessarily. The entry would feature a picture or two with the person (again with permission) and perhaps something related to my Coffee Break (sabbatical).

Some of my guests were confident I would have nothing to write about when it was their turn. On the contrary! Those were the ones I had to heavily edit to keep my word count down.

Additionally, some of my invitees had to be reassured that my intention was not to interview them. Those were often the lunches where we talked for multiple hours. Our conversations bounced from subject to subject without prompting or guidance.

This book captures two themes that intersect with the lunches. First, connection is the most obvious theme that one would ascertain from weekly lunches. The opportunity to meet, converse, and share is clear and understood.

The second theme is that time is a precious resource. The stories in that section are universally relatable. The intersection of these two themes shines the light on a moment when two (or more) people sat down, perused a menu, ordered a drink, exhaled, and began to talk.

Human connection is universal. The diverse personalities and traits captured in this book are also a universal theme. Anyone who reads this memoir will identify with knowing someone compassionate, driven, goofy, a music nerd, a wise sage, etc. Therefore, at the end of each chapter, I include a Wrap-Up, much like a restaurant's to-go box with additional personal stories or nuggets learned.

Spoiler alert: I was not able to secure a new role at Starbucks Coffee Company after my sabbatical concluded. Therefore, my plan to have fifty-two lunches during my year-long Coffee Break was extended. The nine additional lunches (or dinners) provided an opportunity to connect with those I had not been able to schedule in my original plans.

These unanticipated opportunities were timely and proved to be a gift in one case. For someone like me who thrives on goals or challenges, the nine unanticipated encounters were precisely a bonus feature or extra points.

Unfortunately, I was unable to include all sixty-one lunches in this book. However, the additional entries can be found on my website: heatherlcleary.com.

The Big Lunch

Curious if there was any information about whether others have done what I did, I researched the value of people dining together. Is there a psychological impact, social aid, or health benefit?

Many of the articles I encountered dealt with the importance that lunches provide for a person looking to move up the corporate ladder. I was the complete opposite. I wanted nothing to do with the corporate ladder when I was on Coffee Break. I yearned for connection.

In my research, I discovered a study from Oxford University published in 2017 that explored the impact and consequences of dining with others versus dining alone.[1] The results were not all that surprising. People feel connection, a sense of community, and even a deepening of relationships when dining with others.

---

[1] R. I. M. Dunbar, "Breaking Bread: The Functions of Social Eating—Adaptive Human Behavior and Physiology," SpringerLink, March 11, 2017, https://link.springer.com/article/10.1007/s40750-017-0061-4.

What fascinated me about this study was how they interacted with their subjects. In the United Kingdom, during the first weekend in June, cities, communities, and private homes host what is known as The Big Lunch. Individuals gather for the common purpose of sharing one meal.

There is a long history preceding the 2009 Big Lunch. The first known "street parties" began in 1919 with Peace Teas, which were held for children to celebrate the end of World War I.

Subsequent similar events were held to commemorate royal events or joyful national occasions. Unfortunately, after the end of World War II, these gatherings began to wane and with it, community connection.

Enter The Eden Project. Founded in 2009, this United Kingdom-based charity focuses on community outreach at small and large levels. "The Eden Project is an educational charity and social enterprise. We create gardens, exhibitions, art, events, experiences, and projects that explore how people can work together—and with nature—toward a better future. We are inspired by the belief that people are more than capable of changing things for the better, and through creating Eden, we've learnt what ingenuity, resourcefulness, hope, and determination can do."[2]

From its inception, the Eden Project began exploring ways to halt or slow social fragmentation and reconnect people at the neighborhood level. That same year, an idea of "What if, on one

---

[2] "The Big Lunch 2025," Eden Project Communities, April 16, 2025, https://www.edenprojectcommunities.com/the-big-lunch.

day a year, people came together with their communities and shared a meal?" materialized: The Big Lunch.

Gatherings can range from a handful of people in a private home setting to under 100 in a park, to thousands in a city. Since its reincarnation in 2009, some facts and data were gathered, because much like my lunches, this was also a challenge!

- Longest Big Jubilee Lunch: an 800-meter picnic table at the Long Walk, Windsor Castle. The Earl and Countess of Wessex joined thousands at a bring-your-own Big Jubilee Lunch.

- Close second: Morecambe Bay, 5,000 people at 2,500 feet of seafront tables.

- Biggest Big Lunch: Ten thousand people came together at a massive multicultural celebration in Preston.

- In London, the former Prince of Wales and Duchess of Cornwall joined a special Big Jubilee Lunch for 400 guests at the iconic Oval Cricket Ground.

- Most westerly event: a huge picnic at Enniskillen Castle, Northern Ireland.

- Most northern event: The Shetland Isles, where the whole community came together for an intergenerational Big Jubilee Lunch.

- In Wales, events big and small took place from Criccieth to Cowbridge, Llanharry to Llanidloes.

During the 2016 Big Lunch gathering, researchers from Oxford University posed questions to 2,000 people over eighteen years old. In addition, demographic data was also collected.

Questions included how many meals the individual ate alone in a week, how frequently they ate meals with different members of their extended network, how satisfied the respondent was with life, and how many close family members and friends they could depend on for emotional, social, and financial support (if needed).

The individuals were asked to recall the last time they ate a meal with someone other than a person they lived with, and rate how connected they felt to that person(s) after the meal, with zero (0) being "not at all" and ten (10) being "a great deal."

Finally, there was a yes/no choice for whether any of the following occurred during that meal: laughter, reminiscences, jokes, singing, dancing, party games, drinking alcohol, or eating chocolate.

In thinking about my own dining experiences with others, chances are highly likely that I would also respond with the same or similar top four variables: 1) laughter, 2) alcohol, 3) reminiscences, and 4) jokes. My lunches were no different: a lot of laughter, reminiscences, and some alcohol. Although I might substitute jokes for tearful topics (memories? discussions?).

The Big Lunch study provided no insight as to why the concepts of sadness or crying were not explored in the research. It could be to keep a bend toward a more positive experience with fewer gray areas.

As you will read in the forthcoming chapters, I discovered that, in addition to levity, the courage to delve into the area of sadness does bring individuals closer. The vulnerability of one or both diners does have a certain connectedness that happy moments alone cannot forge.

Put differently, from my sixty-one lunches reference point, you cannot have a close or supportive relationship with someone without *all* the emotions.

On July 2, 2018, I began my year-long Coffee Break.

PART I:

HUMAN CONNECTION

Irreplaceable

CHAPTER 1

DARING TO PURSUE A DREAM

"If it is still in your mind, it is worth taking the risk."

–Paulo Coelho

There were two goals I had as a seventeen-year-old. I wanted to attend college to become a French teacher—a practical goal. I also wanted to find a university that offered a dance program—a hobby goal.

The latter goal created a big obstacle. My formal dance education consisted of one year of ballet when I was eight. Over the years, I instead taught myself and developed a passion for dance. I clung to the belief that I had "raw talent" and could pursue that passion in college.

During my senior year of high school, I ventured down the path to find a college or university with a dance theatre program that also offered French as a major. This was not an easy process. Some colleges would have one and not the other. Some universities had many more students than I was comfortable being around.

Then, one fortuitous fall evening at a college fair night, I found the ideal university. I was elated when I met the admissions counselor for Slippery Rock University (SRU). She explained that SRU offered both my desired degree and a dance theatre program, as well as a smaller student population. For the record: yes, Slippery Rock University is a *real* university, and yes, in 2019, Dr. Phil McGraw had to publicly apologize for doubting the institution's existence.

When I was introduced to the SRU Dance Theatre program, I knew my untrained ability fit squarely in the modern/contemporary genre. During my freshman year, I auditioned for a few choreographers.

My self-belief in my talent was quickly validated when one of the lead seniors selected me to be a dancer in her piece. As the lone freshman, I danced with other students who were older, had more training, and were more accomplished than I was. My nickname could have been "sponge" as I was learning as much as I possibly could.

By my sophomore year, I had participated in one professional dance theatre production. I had also modified my degree from French education to International Business with a French minor. Growth and change were everywhere I looked.

The university's dance theatre program encouraged and expected students to step into the role of choreographer. This intrigued me. While I gave it the "ol' freshman try" my first year to be a choreographer, my piece was not selected for the professional stage.

Where others might have been discouraged, this left me more determined in my sophomore year. I had a better understanding of what I needed to do. I was undaunted and not the least bit intimidated by the other dancers, many of whom began formal dance training at the age of three.

I knew, and, more importantly, believed in my abilities. It was easy to visualize dancers, lifts, movements, entrances, exits, spacing, etc. Although I may not have had the formal vocabulary, I trusted that I could demonstrate what was needed to the dancers.

As my sophomore year began, I was in a friend's car on the way to the mall. We were listening to the musician Seal's debut album, *Seal*. The big movements in my piece came to life in my mind as I listened to his melodic, soothing, and creative voice. Though we were not permitted to use music with lyrics per our dance department chair, that album became my co-creator.

I became more emboldened and set my sights higher. After I decided to choreograph a second time, I set up tryouts, explained expectations, secured rehearsal space, and selected dancers.

Headwinds always occur when pursuing a dream that can be stressful. Sometimes, though, they come from the most unexpected of places. The process and rehearsals were well underway when my friends chided me, "Why would you do this?" Or "This is so stressful on you; you should quit." Sidenote: I no longer maintain friendships with any of the doomsayers.

The stress came from having dancers not adhere to my rules and from my large school workload. However, as is my nature, I would not be discouraged. Instead, I doubled down. I released three dancers from the piece, pivoting from a group of six dancers to four, including adding myself as a performer. My stress eased more when I found instrumental music to use.

The day came to audition my piece "The Joy of ..." in front of the department chair and two dance professors. This group ultimately decided who would make the cut for the professional dance theatre production in the spring. Nervously, I waited for feedback and a decision.

"I love this!" said the department chair. "I can see this on the stage."

I was in!

We rehearsed. Selected costumes. Marked the dance on the performance stage. Did all the seemingly normal steps that led up to a dance production. I tried my best to appear calm, collected, and professional, but inside I was over the moon!

A day or two before the show, during dress rehearsal, one of the dance professors walked up to me. I am short, barely 5' 2", so he towered over me in both stance and stature. "Heather," he began, "you have *no right* to be on this stage."

I blanched. I had never heard his voice be so booming or authoritative. He was usually a gentle giant. I began to stutter out that the department chair said my piece was good enough, etc., etc., grasping for anything to defend myself.

He softened, a smile lifting his face and moving his curly hair, "I have spent the last thirty years studying dance. Sweated, learned, did all I could. You have zero years of experience, and you can put *that* piece on a professional stage?! I am both irked and envious! Well done!"

I nearly fainted. It was the highest compliment I had received in my brief life. In that moment, I was validated both externally and internally. I didn't listen to the noise of doubt and disbelief. I forged ahead.

Years later, I continue to dream and have aspirations that some see as ridiculous. I am undeterred; there is something in the challenge. My experience in college is likely why I continue to be drawn toward visionaries and dreamers, and I did not hesitate to set up lunch with some I know and admire.

When I think about the word "visionaries," I hear the Home Depot ad voice saying, "How doers get things done." There is an element of truth to that statement. Projects and goals are about how doers (visionaries, dreamers, and risk-takers) get/got/are getting things done. Some have put their plans into action, resulting in successes like Toby's winery, Ngoc's spa, or Rochelle's small businesses. Or Liz with her art and writing.

These are the people who are risk-takers and adventure seekers. The ones who eschew a "no" for "let's see if it will perhaps work this way." Or the ones who know that hard work and a disciplined way are the only paths to certain success.

These are the people I enjoy being around, am inspired by, and want to emulate. Have they stumbled, fallen, or failed? Absolutely. Did they keep their chin up and their eyes forward on the goal? Without a doubt. That latter part is what endears me to them. It makes me want to be like them, learn from them, and seek my own uncomfortable boundaries.

Liquid Lunch

My "liquid lunch" with Toby defines a person who is a vision-ary with a steady and hard-working eye on a future goal. Back in 2007, Toby was my next-door neighbor.

We shared the experience of doors rotating with elemen-tary school-aged kids tumbling in or out, going through the same moments of changes, never-ending shoe replacement for growing feet, and fall purchases of crayons, safety scissors, glue, and paper.

A couple of years later, Toby met Chris, her true companion or top mischief maker, as she likes to call him (such a fine term). She and her crew moved to another town nearby. We loosely kept in touch either through social media or a professional work app.

As a result of the 2008-2009 recession, I learned that Toby had lost her job in medical sales. For part of her separation pack-age, she was offered the opportunity to take classes in a new or different profession. She elected to learn viticulture at the local community college.

Her classes involved all that is necessary for creating wine. Slowly and methodically, she began making her own wine from other wineries' grapes. She realized she had a knack, talent, and appreciation for what was required. It was at that time that she and Chris started Ducleaux Cellars.

Soon, it became apparent that Toby's dream was too big for the west side life of Washington state. She and her head mis-chief maker, Chris, pulled up their stakes, relocated, and took a chance on Ducleaux Cellars, which included their own vineyard in Eastern Washington.

Much like an aging wine, her vision matured and grew with time and care. She was in the final year of completing her viticulture degree at Walla Walla Community College. This was where we had lunch. Or as she and I quickly called it, our "liquid lunch."

She took my husband and me for a tour of the college's vineyard to her block of green-leafed vines. We walked along the soil, among the thriving branches extending their spiny, finger-like limbs along the well-trained path of wires.

Looking over the delicate tendrils and minute grape clusters the size of my fingernail, I learned from Toby and her instructor, who joined us, about the efforts to grow the vines pesticide-free and let nature do its work from the ground up.

Our lunch continued into the classrooms and testing labs, where Brix statistics are captured. Brix statistics determine the sugar content of the fermenting grapes. Eventually, this determines the alcohol percentage in the bottle of wine.

The tour descended a flight of stairs to a library that was devoid of books. It was the library of wines from past and current students, many of whom now owned and operated their full-fledged wineries.

As I looked at the library contents, I wondered about the past students. Did they envision a winery while they were studying? Are they now living a life beyond their wildest expectations?

The campus is complete with a small-batch production area. Craning my neck, I saw the stainless-steel towers where hoppers feed the clusters into a press with the scent of grapes in the air. Finally, there was a processing and barreling area with oak casks from America, France, and Hungary.

The liquid lunch concluded in the college's tasting room. The tasting flights featured the wines from current students. As we sipped on the offerings, noticing aroma, color, and tasting notes, we chatted about different grapes we preferred.

It is always easy to begin with the simple preference for red versus white. It was fascinating to hear her explain the different growing years that were better for wine production than others. A temperature swing can impact grape growth, harvest, and production, as can smoke from wildfires. She expounded all the components that need to merge to deliver a smooth merlot, a bright cabernet sauvignon, or a complex Super Tuscan.

Although this was not a typical sit-down lunch with plates, forks, knives, and spoons, we still had the opportunity to talk about other life events. I said, "How are your girls doing?"

She excitedly declared, "Can you believe my youngest daughter is about to graduate from high school?" Her daughter and my son had been good friends when they were in the same kindergarten class. It felt like eons ago. I caught her up on all I had been doing while on my Coffee Break.

Listening and watching Toby delight in her newfound livelihood and life made me ponder my own dreams, visions, and personal expectations. Am I where I want to be in my personal life?

I had many questions and precious few answers. Toby inspired me to find more answers and have fewer questions. Unless that question is "Which red wine do I drink tonight?"

Small Business Lunch

I believe that some people accidentally show up in my life. While I was heading down one path, it closed off, and suddenly a new person was in my life. My friend Ngoc (pronounced knock) is such a person—a small business owner who became a friend.

Ngoc and I met through a referral when my esthetician Marissa decided to leave her job to further her education. "Don't worry," Marissa said, "Ngoc is a sweet person and a dear friend. You'll love her!" Oh, how right she was!

Ngoc now operates Studio Spa NW, a thriving business with loyal patrons. This is in no small part due to how she treats each client. She remembers seemingly small details about me, like my birthday (by always sending me a Shemar Moore "Happy Birthday" greeting text), or she can zero in on my mood, like when I am cranky.

During my appointments, she's seen me when the stress of my job literally showed in every pore of my body or when I was on the verge of tears. More often than I care to admit, Ngoc would pause during my appointment and say, "Heather, are you sure your job is the right one for *you*?"

Doing all I could not to let the waterworks leak out, I would take a deep breath, "Perhaps you might be right." It was as if she sensed the source of my sour attitude was work-related.

In those moments, she often recommended a facial to help me out. I realized this had less to do with her business and more with a way she could offer to ease my stress, as only a friend can.

Of course, she also saw me while I was on my Coffee Break. I became practically a whole new client for her. Suddenly, I had low stress levels, smiled more, was happy, and the list goes on and on. "Look at how you smile, Heather! Where are you traveling to next?"

For many years, as Ngoc and I would talk during my appointment, one of us would invariably say, "We need to have lunch one of these days."

Finally, during my Coffee Break, I said, "That's it. We are having lunch!" She laughed and agreed.

We settled at the table to eat our salad lunches on a cool winter day close to Christmas. Ngoc and I discussed her being a small business owner of a personal spa services business.

I said, "Do you realize how many different business locations I have been to with you since I became your client?"

Since I've known her, she has made a few attempts to work for other businesses. This usually involved renting a space at a salon or other personal care location.

"Heather," she said pointedly, "As the saying goes: 'It is often better to work for yourself.'"

Our lunch was a relaxed opportunity to sit, talk, and BE. Naturally, our conversation steered toward our children. "How are Nolan and Bridget?" Her face lit up as she asked. I gave details about their school and swim clubs—normal commentary for me.

When I finished my updates, I asked her, "How is your daughter?" She is a mom of an elementary school child. I love hearing the stories of how her daughter is growing and becoming her own person. I found myself laughing, remembering the days when my children were that age.

"What is it this week?" I asked with a wink. "Does she want to live with you for the rest of her life or something else?"

I do my best to try to keep up with the ever-changing decision that her daughter wants to live with Ngoc for the rest of her life, or that her daughter wants to have her own home. "This week she wants to live with me … *forever!*"

It warms my heart to see a mother so in love with her daughter. We all are, and yet, with Ngoc, I swear there is a little something extra.

We talked about traveling, politics, and being a small business owner. She is smart and purposeful with how she manages her business, which is no easy feat, being the sole proprietor. She protects her time with her daughter by being closed on Sundays and Mondays. I imagine it can't be easy, yet she makes it look effortless.

As our time together continued, I found myself admiring her ease. "You never seem stressed about your business," I told her. Then thinking to myself, *I can't foresee myself being a small business owner, yet if I found the right opportunity, I would seek Ngoc's help and advice.*

Ngoc reminds me of what it means to dream and work hard to see that dream become a reality every day. She inspires and encourages me with my own dreams. When I think of her or talk with her, I can't help but see the dreamer in myself. It makes pursuing my goals a little less scary.

Just Be Lunch

Each week, I looked forward to meeting with my lunch guest for a variety of reasons. I did my best to savor the fleeting moments while sitting across from someone and hearing how their week, day, or month was going, catching up on old times, or simply listening to them. My lunch with Rochelle was no different.

Rochelle and I were introduced at a jewelry party. This was not the typical catalog-based, "why don't you be a salesperson for us" show. No. I met Rochelle, the owner of "Just Be Jewelry," at an event featuring *her* handcrafted jewelry.

Her wares were intricate and distinct pieces of jewelry. Not one for the basics of adding beads to metal, Rochelle learned different methods, such as silversmithing, because she wanted to try something difficult to learn. This knowledge helped her approach to creating a unique line of products.

The fleur-de-lis is Rochelle's symbol for her business. This very recognizable symbol means "at one and the same time, religious, political, dynastic, artistic, emblematic and symbolic." This emblem perfectly represents and summarizes Rochelle. She is neither singular nor linear.

Rochelle is honest and real, as well as kind and compassionate. I have seen her curse in one sentence, and, in the next, immediately pivot to ask how someone's family member is feeling. She is the very essence of a beautiful, creative, and genuine human being, all the while encapsulated in an infectious laugh.

When Rochelle has a vision or idea, she tenaciously determines a way to see it to completion. During her jewelry shows, she began seeing more business opportunities.

She realized a percentage of the female population did not easily have access to affordable, fashionable clothing because they wore larger or plus-sized apparel.

Rochelle wanted to change that. She researched how and where to source the clothes. Her creativity helped her find the right looks and options. Naturally, this addition expanded her business's name to "Just Be Jewelry and Clothing."

Some women approach trying on and purchasing new clothing with trepidation, almost loathing. When I attended Rochelle's clothing shows, I was absolutely delighted to watch women of all sizes and shapes approach the garments Rochelle offered. Leaning on her compassion and honesty, Rochelle was skilled in selecting a piece that she knew would work for that specific client.

As we ate lunch at a local taco place, I recalled a time when I witnessed something at one of her shows. "You stepped back and watched as your customer carefully and timidly donned a printed kimono wrap. Instantly, the woman recognized how the clothing complemented her hair, her eyes, and her figure. All of it came together in a heartbeat. I saw you give this woman the necessary space to realize this on her own. It was a great moment."

She beamed. "That is exactly why I do it. I know it isn't easy finding the right clothes. If I can help in some small way, I will."

With her business, Rochelle gets to witness time and again when the butterfly wrapped tightly in her cocoon bursts forth and begins to flap her wings. If I ever need someone to demonstrate to me how to expand a vision and bring it to life, I will seek out Rochelle. She could teach a course!

Our lunch provided a great opportunity to catch up on our daughters. Rochelle has three girls. Her middle one is the same age as my daughter. As we talked, I was convinced that an instant sisterhood occurs when raising a teenage daughter. I have an ally in Rochelle. I am fortunate to share my joys, worries, concerns, and thoughts with her. She understands because she also has similar reflections.

My lunches allowed me to discuss more involved and sensitive topics. She and I spent the time discussing the concept "Life is short: buy the shoes, eat the chocolate." Several years ago, her cousin Jeff, also my friend, died unexpectedly. His death affected us both deeply. The topic of his passing surfaced as we ate our meals.

It was interesting how the entire world grew quiet as we softly talked about that heartbreaking moment. Wiping tears from our eyes, we didn't need to say a whole lot. We both understood the sorrow the other person felt. One day, he rode the train with me to work, and the next, he wasn't on it. The clanging noise from the service counter brought us back to reality.

While she was busy with her life and her business, Rochelle was also focused on making the moments count. I completely supported this by hearing what she had to say and observe.

Even before Jeff died, she understood that we are not promised our tomorrows or even the end of the day. Each day is meant to be appreciated and enjoyed, even in the darkest of moments. If nothing more than that, there is hope; even in bleak times, someone will see the support and love that surrounds them.

Rochelle is the friend I wish lived next door to me when I want to talk over a cup of coffee. In the tapestry that is my life, Rochelle adds the embellishments and sparkles. She draws my eyes to the beauty that is within me and brings it out with an exclamation point! Her humanity is beyond compare. She lives life every day with the intention (often verbalized) of "JUST BE KIND TO EACH OTHER, DAMMIT!"

As we wrapped up our lunch, I understood that Rochelle helps me see my value inside and then, with her vision and fortitude, brings it to life. My mantra is *Run. Write. Dream. BE.*

Rochelle may have the better approach—Just BE.

Writer Lunch

Elizabeth was a woman who helped me live by most of my mantra: *Run. Write. Dream. BE.*

We met when she worked as the administrative assistant for my vice president at Starbucks. I loved her no-nonsense attitude. Smart and pragmatic are her two most prominent features, even though you might get a glimpse of her colorful tattoos first.

Luckily for me, I have a big mouth. I mentioned one time in a meeting Elizabeth and I attended that I enjoyed writing. Her ears perked up, and we became chummy from that moment.

When I passed by her desk, we often compared our writing notes. "What are you working on right now?" I asked.

She grinned and replied, "The beginning of my memoir."

In Elizabeth, I found a writing ally, though I believe that more importantly, I gained a friend.

Elizabeth came to me one day and told me how she was working toward her editorial certification. As she explained the curriculum, it sounded fascinating to me. I tried to envision myself in that role, taking people's work and recrafting it through suggestions or guidance. Of course, it was quite the romantic notion in my mind. She said, "Maybe someday I can edit your fiction book if you get to that point."

She knew that when I took my Coffee Break, I planned to utilize some of the time to work on writing a fiction book about women in rock and roll. She had mentioned her singing background once or twice. I suspected that her musical experience would prove useful, especially when it came to editing.

While I had started the story during the first part of my Coffee Break, filling in the colors, words, and ideas was a TOTALLY different process. It took me much longer than I had anticipated to get her anything of substance to edit.

Life got in the way. Focus got out of the way. All the while, my patient friend Elizabeth waited, understanding and supportive through the entire process. It was a happy day when I called and asked her for editing services. She edited the first four chapters.

She approached the work with professionalism and offered insight throughout the process, providing comments and suggestions. Her musical background proved to be very helpful, though I teased her that her cruelest advice required me to add song lyrics to my book. Ugh. That was not easy.

Although I had not known her for long when we discussed her editorial coursework, I noticed a clear increase in her confidence. She sat taller in her chair and appeared more assured.

I love it when I see someone realizing their dreams; it is infectious. Dreamers make me dream, too. Little did I know then that her writing vision of creating Memoirtistry® was in the incubation stages.

Our lunch was a great time to catch up after not seeing each other for several months. Though we often texted or followed each other on social media, it was clearly not enough for either of us. As we nibbled on our Cuban sandwiches with the tangy aioli, the time flew by.

Elizabeth quickly admitted her life had not been a traditional one. When I listened to her tell her life stories, I realized she was an enchantress of sorts. My only choice was to BE present to listen to her.

She brought me into her world with the words she selected. Her vocabulary was not excessive or condescending. Instead, she wove senses and emotion into the stories. I was enraptured as the sun coming in through our window seats warmed me.

Further, I often appreciated how she listened to me when I talked. She leaned in, paused, and maintained eye contact. That last part was crucial for me when I talked with someone.

Determined, I wanted to hear more during our lunch about her writing journey. She was also working on her memoir. Even with the differences between fiction (me) and nonfiction (her) as we talked, I understood that the process was still the same.

"Here is how it works, Heather," she said. "Formulate an idea. Begin to build an outline. Color in the details. I realized that the crafting of my book all fell into place when I figured out how to break my idea into a more manageable format."

I was excited to learn more about where she was heading with her writing career outside of her book. "The next step in my journey will be to work as a content writer," she said. "I have some creative ideas for freelance work."

Fast forward to today. Watching her dreams materialize into Memoirtistry®, a writing, editing, and artistic support service, has been my true honor.

I am fortunate to have someone like Elizabeth in my life. She helps me realize my potential. (*Write.*) She can also see my vision for the path ahead. (*Dream.*) She not only walks beside me on my journey but also has the skills to get me there patiently. (*BE.*)

Listening to Elizabeth during lunch, I recalled a quote I hold dear:

*"And the day came when the risk to remain tight in a bud
was more painful than the risk it took to blossom."*
~Anaïs Nin

The Wrap-Up

When I was a child of six or so, I read all the different book installments from the "Value Tales Series" by Spencer Johnson. I would race to the children's section at my local public library to see if there was a new title or check out a book I had previously read. For hours on end, I would read and reread the oversized white books with the colorful caricatures drawn in big, thick designs on the cover.

With titles like *The Value of Determination: The Story of Helen Keller, The Value of Imagination: The Story of Charles Dickens, The Value of Helping: The Story of Harriet Tubman,* or *The Value of Courage: The Story of Jackie Robinson,* it is little wonder that throughout my entire life, dreamers and visionaries fascinated me. Their stories came to life on the pages and in my mind. I read about how their bold actions, quiet planning, hard work, and focused dedication to their individual goals all brought them to the forefront of history.

Those books gently eased me into the stories and tales I would read as a young adult with more difficult topics, such as those of Anne Frank, Sojourner Truth, and Maya Angelou. They too required courage, determination, and imagination to live their lives. Gone were the cute cartoon drawings. Still, I knew that if I wanted to learn about them, I had to be willing to read their words or stories.

Whether it is pluck or moxie, something endearing connects me to a person who dares to dream and is courageous enough to take that first step.

The lunches in this chapter took me back to my youth, as I read about people with bold ideas and determined focus. Each of my lunch guests envisioned for themselves a world beyond corporate America. Their work, toil, and labor are continuous. Yet, I saw a freedom in their eyes when they talked about their business. Or a thrill in their voice when they spoke about an expansion.

Whether they got dirt under their fingernails, callouses on their hands, cramps in their wrists, or tightness in their neck, they are all living a dream they designed.

CHAPTER 2

MORE THAN A PAYCHECK

"The strength of the team is each individual member.
The strength of each member is the team."

–Phil Jackson

In the late 1990s, I worked for a small national bookstore chain based in Dallas, Texas, called Half Price Books, a brick-and-mortar retailer offering new and used books. It was my favorite job I've ever had. I found moments of pure Zen while shelving books and thrived with the challenge of buying books from the public.

A person could bring in a single box or several boxes of books. It was my job to look at the books, assess their condition, understand the current inventory, and determine the potential selling price.

Used books, except for collector's items, were at least half the listed price. Once I had reviewed the entire lot, I would provide the customer with a non-negotiable offer price. The customer could decline the offer and retrieve their books, or accept it for either store credit or cash.

One day, I was working at the book buying counter. A woman in her forties came in with a few boxes of mixed book types—hardback, trade paper, and mostly mass-market paperbacks (the little ones). I opened the boxes, inhaling the familiar scent of older books. The entire lot was from the science fiction genre.

I noted that none of the titles were popular or from trending authors. Apart from a handful of books, they would immediately go to the clearance shelves for twenty-five or fifty cents. I assumed this was obviously a standard "buy," with someone trying to purge some books from a home collection.

Not anticipating anything out of the ordinary, I stood across the buying counter and presented the woman with her cash offer. She immediately burst into tears. A bit embarrassed, I blanched and braced to prepare my explanation on the value, popularity of the books, clearance, etc.

As I began my standard "This is how we make an offer" speech, she shook her head and looked at me with small, clear lakes in her eyes.

"No," she said as she cleared her throat, "it's not the amount. It's that …," closing her eyes as if conjuring the strength that had betrayed and left her. "These were my younger brother's … in his home. He died from cancer, and I didn't know what to do with them …" She exhaled the sentence as if it were a single word.

More composed and confident, she continued, "I don't read science fiction. And there are so many of them. I … I …"

I took her hesitation as a signal to swiftly move from behind the counter to be fully face-to-face with her. I carefully and gently looked into her eyes, took a deep breath to conjure my resolve, and quickly prayed for the right words.

I explained, "You clearly came to the perfect place. Your brother obviously loved these books, as evidenced by the cracked spines and soft edges on the covers. I promise that when I put these on the shelves, someone who loves science fiction as much as your brother did will find these books. That person will be grateful for their new stash. They will take the books home and appreciate them as your brother once did. His legacy will live on."

She blinked and softly smiled at me. I paused, near tears myself. As soon as it felt appropriate, I walked back behind the counter and printed her offer. Returning to face her again, I handed her the paper. "Are you okay to drive?"

She exhaled again. "Yes, I am okay." As she walked away, I appreciated the moment as a learning lesson. *You never know what someone else is going through.*

That memory was seared into my mind. I often reminisced on this story as an example of managing an awkward situation for a job interview question. Or even when I saw a science fiction paperback at my local Half Price Books.

About ten years later, when reading Carlos Ruiz Zafón's book *The Shadow of the Wind*, I encountered an eerily fitting passage: "Every book, every volume you see has a soul. The soul of the person who wrote it, and the soul of those who read it and lived and dreamed it. Every time a book changes hands, every time someone runs his eyes down its pages, its spirit grows and strengthens."[3] I immediately recalled the memory and felt gratitude for providing that woman with comforting words.

This story was often retold during my lunches, especially when the topic of favorite jobs came up.

Military Advocate

From a very young age, I can remember poring over my dad's photos from his time in the Vietnam War. I was fascinated by these mysterious people within the confines of the square photograph. The white outline contrasted with the scenes, mostly the familiar drab green of Army life.

Some veterans from any war are reluctant to share their experiences. My dad was not one of these. He willingly discussed his wartime service.

Sitting on the floor with the pictures splayed out in front of me, my dad filled my head with stories about this guy or that: hometowns, what their moms would send in care packages, and whether they had a girlfriend, wife, or even a child at home. Many of the photographs were taken of the guys in my dad's hooch (the tent the guys called "home" in the middle of the jungle in a foreign country).

My dad told me his stories long before I would have had history lessons at school that taught me about the Vietnam War. Instead, my dad, a U.S. Army draftee, posed as my instructor.

---

[3] Carlos Ruiz Zafón, *The Shadow of the Wind*, (2001), 5

As I grew, he stressed the importance of understanding what it meant to be a veteran since his father (my grandfather, drafted in WWII) and my great-grandfather (WWI) were veterans too.

Growing up in Pennsylvania, we lived about four hours from Washington, D.C., close enough for us to easily travel to see the Vietnam Veterans Memorial Wall.

When anything related to the Vietnam War came to our hometown, we were front and center with the activities. I understood at a young age that the Vietnam veterans were not greeted with the fanfare and glory that other wartime veterans received.

My dad would look down at me and say in his serious tone, "Heather, if you ever meet a Vietnam veteran, I want you to shake their hand and say, 'Welcome home.'" I did not really understand what that meant until much later in my life.

Supporting veterans became second nature to me. My husband, Mark, an Army veteran, served in one of three peacetime eras in the entire history of the United States. For a sliver of time in the mid-1980s, the United States was not at war with anyone.

Unfortunately, this meant that for a very long time, Mark was not recognized as a "full veteran" in the eyes of some organizations. I always encouraged him to take pride in his service. We were not at war then. That didn't mean he wasn't ready in the event one started. Recently, he has begun to be prouder of his service and is comfortable sharing his experiences.

My brother served in the Air Force. He helped several of our cousins see the benefits that military life in the Air Force could mean for them. I have been surrounded by active-duty military servicemen or veterans for my entire life. I thought that was normal. It wasn't until a fortuitous day at work that I learned this was not true for everyone.

One random day in 2009, while I worked at Starbucks Corporate, I received an email from a fellow Sourcing teammate. The son of a supplier had been deployed and was struggling with both his own morale and that of his unit. The mom wondered if we could send him some coffee, a small reminder of home. It was a simple ask.

My teammate sent a note to everyone in Sourcing and some random Supply Chain individuals. The outpouring was immediate and mind-blowing. She received a multitude of colorful bags of coffee, worn paperback books, sports magazines, candy, cookies, and personal letters. She had started with a small box on her desk; however, she quickly claimed an empty cubicle to fill with all the donated items.

A seed of an idea was quietly germinated. Since the empty cubicle was nearly bursting, my teammate wisely began to write down the names of other soldiers we knew were deployed. These were the early days of what became known as the Military Packing Parties.

I jumped in with both feet to help my teammate, asking her what I could do to support her. When she read my heartfelt, handwritten letter to the soldiers, she understood my dedication to this cause. "Help me pack boxes," she exclaimed!

Oh, the early days—the learning curve of how to fill out the dreaded customs forms. We quickly learned that we needed one or two people solely dedicated to completing the forms (usually the last person to arrive at the lunchtime packing party).

The noise of packing tape still rings in my ears, along with the familiar waft of coffee from multiple one-pound bags being carefully added and the chatter of the six or eight people stuffing everything else into the U.S. Post Office's red, white, and blue boxes.

Soon, we had lists of what the soldiers would like: hot chocolate and tea for the non-coffee drinkers, books, etc. By a stroke of luck, we were able to partner with the Girl Scouts and send their cookies! What a taste of home; the familiarity of the green dot on a coffee bag, along with the well-recognized Girl Scout cookies.

Our favorite item to send was the soldiers' favorite too—butt wipes! As they told us, "We don't smell very good out here in the desert!" This would always send us into a fit of giggles, yelling "Yo! My box needs more butt wipes!" We might have been a bit too loud at times, as people walking past our conference room would stare in through the windows.

Each month, we would mail the care packages to soldiers in far reaches of the world. We quickly learned the difference between forwarding and not forwarding packages for the soldiers' safety. We learned the rules about not including liquids or pornographic materials in the boxes.

Our favorite lesson learned was that some boxes with the APO (Army/Air Force Post Office) or FPO (Fleet Post Office) addresses would arrive in the promised two or three days! Across oceans and deserts in just two or three days!

I was dedicated each month to this grassroots work. We were an all-volunteer group, including supplying the funds to mail the boxes. When my teammate retired, I picked up her reins and led the packing parties.

The soldiers' names came from teammates or other soldiers leaving their deployment. These names rotated in and out of our list. We always tried to send two boxes to each soldier. That meant we usually packed about thirty-five boxes from twelve to one p.m.

The only item not personally donated was the coffee. Our teammate at the roasting plant would send us the bags marked for donation because they might not have gone through the machine exactly as planned. Each month, Dave (whose lunch is in this chapter) sent us coffee. We quickly became a well-oiled machine.

Even after leaving Starbucks, my military advocacy remains. Now, I focus on helping soldiers with PTSD (post-traumatic stress disorder) through half-marathon races or donations. My support is still evident as it is scattered throughout some of my lunches.

Information Technology (IT) Support Lunch

When I worked at Starbucks Corporate, I had two very different career roles. For the first six and a half years of my tenure, I began in the Beverage Components Sourcing area. I bought all the ingredients that went into lattes and Frappuccinos® except the milk, coffee, and syrups.

Or, as I would easily sum it up for people, I was the "sugar and spice girl." Promotional toppings like chocolate curls—that was me. Cookie crumble topping—that was me as well. My favorite topping to buy was the salt-sugar topping for the salted caramel mocha offered during the holidays.

As fun and exciting as that world appeared, I was more intrigued with the Information Technology side of the business. I found small opportunities that gave me more skills and knowledge needed to move into that realm.

Eventually, a role that required my supply chain experience and IT functionality became available. I acted as the conduit between the IT developers and the supply chain disciplines. I remained in that role until my Coffee Break.

Pamela is one of those people who started as a coworker and quickly became a friend. Though I always had fun telling people how I knew or met her, "Pamela was an IT customer of mine," she would invariably roll her blue eyes or groan when I would say that.

To translate, in the nerdy, geeky IT world she and I worked in, she was one of my Super Users of the system I supported. Lost, bored, or confused? It's okay. Most people's eyes would gloss over. She and I had this inherent awareness that what we did for work was not super exciting to the average individual, much less easy to comprehend.

As goes the way of technology, Pamela and I spent a lot of time together in bland conference rooms huddled around whirling computers, sometimes pumping out enough heat to warm our coffee cups. Therefore, it is understandable that we would naturally talk about other things as we waited for the hourglass or circle to stop spinning on the screen.

We quickly discovered that we had shared passions for music and whiskey. The priority of those depended on the stress level for the day. She and I would talk ad nauseam about a musician from Washington, Allen Stone, who was new to the music scene. He was a favorite of hers at the annual Summer Meltdown Festival. I had learned about him from a friend of mine. We both liked his smooth sound.

I absolutely appreciated, and I know she did as well, the ability to talk shop when we needed. We worked too closely and sat in too many meetings together not to find the need to encourage each other. I am grateful I had her to vent to when needed.

Sometimes, we would huddle in a small conference room to keep the other from screaming about shared frustrations. Or I would rush up four or five flights of stairs to tell her about seemingly small victories because I did not want to send yet *another* Instant Message to someone. Most importantly, in Pamela, I had a comrade when no one else seemed to understand the quirkiness of my world.

She picked the perfect restaurant for our lunch. A small place designed to emulate a "nonsmoking cocktail lounge" known for its amazing happy hour drinks. The ideal place for Pamela and me!

We climbed *up* to our high-top table. Oh, the high-top, the bane of short women's existences! The bright red and black colors and the alternative music playing in the background set us up for a wonderful lunch.

Having spent numerous happy hours together, she couldn't wait to show me this new location. "Heather, this place has the *best* Greyhounds I have ever had!" A greyhound is a mixed drink comprised of vodka and grapefruit juice. Of course she was right.

My BLT plus avocado sandwich absolutely warranted a picture! Such an annoying trend that I love to do! The smell of the perfectly cooked, crispy bacon set my taste buds into overdrive. The smartly sliced green avocado mostly hid the red tomato and green bib lettuce. The sandwich, served open-faced on toasted sourdough bread, was perfectly crunchy. What a tremendous meal!

I couldn't wait to hear about her last-minute trip to Disneyland. With that familiar Disney twinkle in her eye, she said, "I think it all went down from thought to planning to walking into the park with my Mickey Mouse ears in twelve to sixteen hours. Talk about last minute! I had a wild hair and simply went."

Laughing, I said, "For you to get from Seattle to Anaheim that quickly was no small feat! That spirit is why we are good friends!"

There are moments when we each do something completely unexpected, and while some may scratch their heads, we are yelling "Right on!" to the other. I'm certain if I had known her in high school, we would have been in a LOT of trouble together! Some people come along at better times in your life.

When I reflect on my lunch with Pamela, I am reminded of a phrase I love: "People come into our lives for a reason, a season, or a lifetime." Pamela is in my life to be a sounding board with a bit of pixie dust.

Sista from Another Mista Lunch

Michelle and I refer to each other as our "Sista from another Mista." We started our friendship as I have with many people, working at Starbucks Corporate. We met when we both worked in the Sourcing organization. We became instant friends. Okay, truth be told, add wine = instant friends. I'm joking, well maybe not.

While Michelle and I do enjoy a good glass of red wine, fortunately, that isn't where our sisterhood ends. To maintain a professional and personal connection, we would schedule a monthly touch base coffee, usually at the Starbucks store inside the Starbucks Corporate building. Talk about convenient!

For thirty or so minutes, we took the time to make sure we knew how the other person's job was going, especially after we each moved to different departments.

Hunched over our small round table as other Partners walked hurriedly past, we would wrap our hands around our mugs, sip on our warm coffee or tea, and provide moral support, encouragement, and even the occasional honest "What were you thinking?" comments. There was something special and comforting about a person who understood your work-related stress.

When one of us interviewed for a new role, the other was in her corner, asking for updates or status on the process. Or even the "Do you need a reference?" question. Although we were friends, we were also familiar with how the other person worked.

It was good to have someone like Michelle in my work world. She was one of the few people whose desk I could drop by for a sanity check and vice versa. When it felt like everything in my job was going wrong and the world had a vendetta against me, Michelle bluntly reminded me, "No, Heather, the *entire world* has not shit on you."

My ray of sunshine. I hope I was the same for her.

When we sat down in our booth, she said how much she enjoyed coming to that restaurant for the quiet ambiance, delicious food, and great drinks. Outside of work, I love talking with Michelle because we don't always have to ruminate about our jobs.

Some of my favorite moments with Michelle are spent talking about traveling. Her trips in years past have been nothing short of wonderful. Whether it was domestic or international travel, Michelle was game to visit somewhere new to her, like Italy.

If we both go missing, I'll give you a hint—look in Tuscany. We are all about the book and movie *Under the Tuscan Sun*. The idea of living a low-stress life in a relatively secluded countryside with an abundance of homegrown food is right for us. Perhaps she and I will move there someday and peddle our olive oil wares at the local farmer's market in the Tuscany region.

I enjoyed watching her light up as she talked about her son, Eric. He, too, was a Starbucks Partner. He worked hard, patiently, and intently, much like his mother. If he had a question, he would ask. If he knew the answer, he would share.

Before I went on Coffee Break, he was one of my loyal IT super users. And (because I know he will read this) NOT one of my troublemakers! Some of my IT super users I called my *problem children.* These were the real pains who were unable to learn, help themselves, or would cry "wolf"—the worst kind. I would groan or cringe when I saw their email question or Instant Message come through.

No, Eric was competent and confident. He asked questions when he didn't know something and understood after the first explanation, which, believe me, was no easy task for the area I supported.

Usually, Michelle and I minimized the talk about work. It was particularly difficult on the day of our lunch, since we both experienced the loss of fellow Starbucks Partners due to recent layoffs.

With a sadness in her downcast eyes, she sat back in her forest green booth seat and said, "I can't believe they laid off so and so. It doesn't make sense."

I shook my head in agreement. "I know. I can't rationalize it either."

In that moment, I looked at her. I think we realized that steering our conversation back to work was inevitable. It did help to talk about the painful stuff, too.

I am proud to say that I am part of a wonderful circle of Michelle's friends. There is a core group of six of us who are close.

There are also side friendships that are very solid. Much like a colorful spirograph (remember those?), the smaller, one-on-one friendships, when combined, create a big, beautiful picture that makes the six of us even closer.

That is an exceptional dynamic. I am not alone when I say I am very fortunate and blessed to know these amazing five women. Their stories are at times uniquely their own and yet similar in a different moment. That allows us to draw upon each other for strength, support, and friendship.

My lunch with Michelle was a reminder of that one person in your life who is more than a friend. Someone who is a soul sister in every sense of the word. She reflects me, protects me, and gently calls me on the carpet when something isn't right. She lets me drink her wine. And unlike some biological sisters, she lets me hang with her friends.

Browser Lunch

When an LSU (Louisiana State University) Tiger alum steps into your ether, your life is going to change. Mine did with Darla.

Technically, when I was not on Coffee Break, Darla and I were teammates, and for lack of a better phrase, partners in crime. We were part of the friendly faces who graciously helped Business Intelligence (not an oxymoron) users with the IT systems we supported for supply chain and retail operations. Darla and I had an unwavering commitment to providing *proper* customer service.

Believe it or not, this occasionally got us into trouble when we would go toe-to-toe with vice presidents or other leaders. We had to fight for various customers' business reporting needs (things like data size, data fields, and even reporting permissions, to name a few). Still, I wouldn't want anyone else united with me in that fight except Darla.

Darla was my sanity in an often bizarre and insane world—ah, technology. Her still-Southern accent endeared me to her even more. Her gentle voice made me smile and made me happy, even when she would say, "Bless your heart, Heather," knowing full well that meant she was frustrated with me.

She had a way of listening when she became still and looked straight at me. Then she offered her wisdom in that same calm and gentle voice. We've shared laughter, tears, and moments of *What the ...* or *You are **never** going to believe this one. The browser that once accepted our platform no longer works with the platform ...*

We swore we were going to get T-shirts printed for our office hours that said, "Eventually succeeded, but encountered and resolved errors." The passive-aggressive T-shirts were safer than all the sarcastic memes we really wanted to wear, such as "I have neither the time nor the crayons to explain this to you" or "Oops, there goes the last shit I gave."

Darla and I were in constant day-to-day interactions, often sitting in the same meetings or working on the same issues, frequently asking users, "Have you tried a different browser?"

To say I miss working with her terribly is an understatement. I miss being there for her. I miss laughing at the dumb jokes. I miss the moments of small victories. I miss our teamwork.

Once, I read that including "team player" on your resume is passé and irrelevant. I completely disagree. If there is one thing I enjoy most, it is working together with a group of individuals as a team. You see the best and sometimes even the most surprising in people. You see their values, ethics, and determination. The team may want to reach a common goal, yet the journey of various individuals makes it so much more human. Teamwork (in my ever-so-humble opinion) is humanity. Humanity is not passé.

Darla's heart and fierce loyalty are what I miss the most every day. Yes, I know I can text or call her at any time, but there is something very different about not seeing her frequently that makes some of my days lonely. I send "cat-ies" (kind of like selfies, except with my cats) to her. She receives pictures of me and my two furry gals snuggled up to me as I attempt to type on my computer. If Darla is working from home, I will get a similar picture of one of her kitties or, when my best canine pal was alive, of her dog, Scooter the Destroyer.

During my Coffee Break, I sent her a text I thought was only reserved for frustrating work conditions. My exasperated text read, "Never on my Coffee Break did I ever think I would *ever* have to have a conversation that went 'You know, it might be your browser not functioning properly.'" She suggested a glass of wine as a remedy for that day. Did I mention that Darla is also brilliant?

I was quite happy to spend the lunch catching up with her face-to-face. Outside of work and her parental obligations, she was full-on into nurturing her dad long-distance. Her father still lives in Baton Rouge. (Geaux Tigers!) He was beginning to slow down and needed a voice of reason.

More often than not, while Darla visited him, it was less about a voice of reason and more about the physical effort to rehab his home and property. The maintenance became too much for him to handle. Darla did what she always does—got in there, no questions asked, no arguments given, and she FIXED IT! (Our little joke referencing a *Saturday Night Live* skit.)

While in Baton Rouge, she sent me pictures of spiders, other creepy crawly things in the far corners of the porch and shed, and wriggling snakes while she attempted to mow the lawn. She did it all. She sweated, toiled, and continued raising herself up as my heroine. Our lunch was pure luck, as she was about to fly to her dad's house that night.

We caught up on all the chaos that work life at Starbucks entailed: layoffs, a Nestlé deal, etc. She and I had been directly impacted by a lot of the big news at the corporate headquarters.

As much as we didn't want to talk about it, having a friend to discuss the less wonderful sides of our world was comforting. Wine therapy is generally what we called it. Or Food Truck therapy. Or the occasional cheese curds at Henry's Restaurant with the other ladies of Business Intelligence therapy.

There were moments when I realized the universe was really in my corner when I had the chance to work every day with someone who truly exemplifies the words partner and team player. It makes it all the better when you can add the word friend.

Grounding Lunch

When I sat at my desk at home, writing while sipping Starbucks coffee from an Air Force mug, I would of course think of my brother, and then my memories would turn to my friend Stephen. We met while I worked at Starbucks; he had also previously served in the Air Force.

We both belonged to a Tuesday night Starbucks bowling league. Let me state for the record that I was the bowler who went for the fun and the beer. Stephen and his team were there to win and have the occasional beer, too.

His team bowled circles around ours. The only hope my Fireballers team had was for a couple of us to have a clutch night, and our handicap score could beat them. Even when that didn't happen, I still ensured we all had fun and tried not to take ourselves too seriously.

When I moved from Sourcing into my role in IT, Stephen also changed teams. He became one of my super users for the IT system I supported.

In that job, I met his alter-ego, "Johnny #5." (Please, please, someone know this!) For those unfamiliar with the reference, Johnny #5 is from the 1980s movie *Short Circuit*. ("Hey, laser lips, your mama was a snow blower!")

Stephen was insanely gifted with Excel. He naturally became Johnny #5. He could design formulas and functions that I swore even tested Microsoft's limits. He pushed his laptop so hard that it required a separate cooling system. To contrast, I basically knew the AutoSum function.

One of the subjects I enjoyed discussing with him was his service in the Air Force. "See the world!" says the recruiter. "Experience other countries!" Or, as it turned out, send Stephen to North Dakota.

His descriptions of the weather and isolation stunned me. Stephen's stories made it seem like there were probably four days total they could ride motorcycles; the rest was spent on snow-mobiles. An exaggeration, I know. Still, it was clear that being stationed at Grand Forks AFB (Air Force Base) created a tight-knit community.

We both have a great appreciation for R&B music. He is much better versed in the lesser-known mainstream songs and musicians. He made it his personal mission to educate me in the world of the O'Jays, the Shining Stars, the Isley Brothers, etc.

Being a music fan, I was open to learning and understanding different songs and musicians. I appreciate friends who take the time to teach me about various genres of music.

Stephen left Starbucks before I did, and while it bummed me out, it was a life-changing decision for him.

We were at Happy Hour one time, and he had a grin on his face that was bigger than I had ever seen. He looked like the cat who swallowed the canary. I said in my best big sister tone, "What is up with you? Why the grin?" (Truth be told, I was rather certain I knew.)

He blushed, and in an uncharacteristically quieter-than-usual voice, he said, "I met someone." Did you ever have a friend say those exact words, and you knew precisely what that meant? Yeah, that was that day.

He proceeded to tell me that he had only known Lynea for about a month. Then he couldn't stop talking. There seemed to be a mix of relief at finally verbalizing his excitement and pure joy at having met Lynea. Being his pseudo big sister, I listened and knew she was *The One*. Yes, even that early on.

From that time on, the three of us spent a few Happy Hours together enjoying our favorite Taylor Shellfish oysters. Fast forward. Yes, I was right! It was a great honor to witness their beautiful May wedding.

For our lunch, he and I picked a traditional Mexican restaurant with bright yellows, reds, blues, and greens. Over the sound of sizzling plates of food, our lunch was a great opportunity to catch up since it had been some time since we last saw each other.

He smiled and said, "I had a blast going back to Maryland and surprising my mom with a birthday party. We all had great fun—dancing, laughing, and celebrating. I'm grateful it worked out."

Surrounded by eclectic tables and chairs, he talked about the careful and intentional future he was building with Lynea. He shared the details of their individual and mutual dreams. It did my heart good to see a friend happy, joyful, and so in love.

Years ago, Stephen taught me to appreciate scotch. Even though we were dining in the hallowed halls where tequila was king, he and I talked for a long time about scotches, whiskeys, and bourbons.

At lunch, I showed him a picture of the birthday presents from my husband: three small-batch and specialty bourbons.

Stephen exclaimed, "You look like Diane Keaton in her happiest moment!"

What a compliment! I have always appreciated Diane Keaton for her work, natural beauty, and gregarious character.

What I appreciate about Stephen is that I can't bullshit him. He knows when I'm happy, upset, frustrated, or elated. Our lunch was no different. He could sense a lot was wrong in my world. It didn't take much effort for me to blurt it all out. "I don't know if I have a job to go back to. I'm worried about … and … and …" He patiently listened.

When I was finished, his advice was "Compartmentalize everything, Heather." Then he proceeded to help me sort all the stress and mess into buckets. Noting that "this one will soon be over" or "you will have to keep slugging through that one." Soon, I felt better.

Stephen sees through my thin veil of armor. He takes the time and energy to educate me. He is that friend who reminds me when life is going sideways to "Sing a Song" like Earth, Wind, and Fire suggests.

Seasoned Veteran Lunch

Since Starbucks gave me the tremendous opportunity of a Coffee Break, it seemed appropriate to have lunch with one of its longest-standing Partners. That meant my good friend, Dave. He has been a Starbucks Partner for over forty years. I am quite sure he has seen and heard it all.

Dave is well known in many Starbucks circles. How could he not be? He started the same day as Howard Schultz. The joke was about who let whom in the door; that was who had more seniority. With some recent retirements, Dave is now the Partner with the most years of service.

We met when I worked in Sourcing, and I made a dumbass error. That may be harsh on me. He worked at the roasting plant warehouse. I had accidentally mistyped the dimensions for the little gingerbread toppings that he was trying to receive into the system. He called me on the phone—it was that urgent—no emails for this issue. He immediately set me straight.

Once the dust settled, I sent him a follow-up Instant Message. It was then that I discovered that he lived about three miles away from me. I offered to buy him a drink as an apology for my goof. The rest is history.

Instantly, he became good friends with my husband and me. Initially, this involved us meeting up at his infamous "man-cave" for poker parties, billiard parties, bonfires, barbecues, after Thanksgiving parties, etc. Along the way, I met a whole host of people who were his friends and quickly became mine.

Over the years, in addition to hanging out with him, he invited my husband and me to join the Starbucks bowling league. Each Tuesday, the Fireballers met up, and while we weren't a stellar team in terms of bowling skills, we were known to have a great time.

We created a random tradition: during the third frame of the second game, we would drink a shot of Fireball. There was no rhyme or reason to it; it was something we all agreed to do.

When my husband cooked for large groups, Dave was right there beside him, prepping, cooking, whatever was needed to make the meals successful. Dave and Mark were a tremendous cooking duo. A person was always in for a treat when those two were behind the grill or stove.

In March 2009, when our supply chain organization began the Military Packing Parties, Dave was the first and most active member. He made sure that every box had ample amounts of coffee.

When I took over the efforts to coordinate the monthly packing parties, Dave was my rock in supporting the troops. He always made sure that I had coffee to send to our deployed soldiers when I needed it.

One of the soldiers we supported sent an American flag as a thank you. It was flown over their military base on the final day of deployment in Afghanistan. I worked with my dad to create a shadow box that would properly display the flag and certificate because that gift needed to be at the roasting plant where Dave worked. In a surprise ceremony, a couple of loyal packing party members and I had the honor to present Dave with that shadow box. He was stunned.

Dave and I met up at one of our favorite wine bars for lunch, which seemed to be a fitting place to celebrate our professional accomplishments and our friendship, too.

We shared an incredible bottle of red wine from the Walla Walla, Washington, wine area. He and I took the time to swirl the red liquid in our rounded glasses. We held it up to the light and saw the clarity. Then we sniffed inside the glass to smell the notes and aromas. A clink of the glasses and our lunch was officially underway. The food was secondary.

Dave and I talked about the current state of Starbucks, how much it has changed in the over twelve years since I started, and the Partners we remembered and the ones who impacted our lives. We talked of the goofballs that we knew would never last, and the incredible ones that did.

As we ate our lunch and drank our wine, we remembered cookouts and parties, old friends, and new ones. Then we wondered where some friends were now. He and I quietly agreed how grateful we were for the ones still in our lives who had a brush with mortality.

Time and distance can separate people. Dedication and intention can bring them back or keep them together. There might have been a couple of tears that welled up in each of our eyes in that moment, although I won't admit that here (wink).

While we ate, Dave told some of the patrons that knew him (this *always* happens. I can't go anywhere with that guy without bumping into an acquaintance!) about the intention behind why we were having lunch.

Eventually, we steered to the subject of music. Somehow, this happens more and more frequently to me, especially the subject of *Yacht Rock: The easy listening music of the '70s and '80s.*

Somehow, from our discussion, we decided to have a Yacht Rock party. There was a "Summer Breeze," while we were "Reminiscing," and perhaps "Brandy" would make an appearance because we all knew she was a *Fine Girl.*

Dave and I talked and talked for hours. It's what we *always* do. We talk. We laugh. We listen. We care. We support. We chide. We believe. We remember. We try to forget. We hope. We worry. We take the time. We do our best to be.

Dave is someone who can absolutely laugh with me while he is laughing at me. He is a person who thinks of others way before he thinks of himself. He was a rock when I needed help with the military packing parties.

I hope to return the same support if he were in need. Dave is the absolute epitome of one of the greatest songs—James Taylor's "You've Got a Friend."

The Wrap-Up

Lunches with teammates and coworkers are a time-honored tradition. Griping over pasta meals or celebrating over sandwiches, there is a connection that occurs. Sometimes, the connections blossom into friendships; others stay purely professional.

During my time at Starbucks Corporate, a swarm of food trucks would line up in front of the building each day. At the height of this, there were four, maybe five options to select.

The food trucks provided an opportunity to get outside, sometimes braving the elements, to breathe fresh air or smell the aromas coming from the barbecue truck or the Hawaiian/Korean fusion food truck. For some people, it was the only time they left their desks for something other than meetings or a restroom break.

There were times when I went by myself. The wonderful part was that even if I stood in line by myself, I was never alone. None of us were. People would strike up conversations with the person in front of or behind them.

Small connections were everywhere. Easy conversations like "What is your favorite item on the menu?" turned strangers into acquaintances, especially when I would see that person the next week and excitedly say, "Thanks for the recommendation on the number seven! That was delicious!"

With some of my friends, we had favorite trucks, like on Fridays, when the quinoa bowl truck came. It offered gluten-free options, so one of my teammates and I would always eat at that one.

Lacking originality, we always ordered the exact same options each week. Mine was always the Sunshine Bowl: Warm quinoa and white beans with red bell peppers, broccoli, carrots, feta, green onions, pumpkin seeds, and a lemon turmeric sauce. No matter the time of year, that bowl would always satiate my lunchtime cravings.

When we had a group of contractors, on Tuesdays, we would arrange our schedules to go to the falafel food truck together. Since there was always a long line, we tried to go before the rush of people or after.

As we inched forward in the slowly moving queue, we would talk about the IT system we were upgrading or how our families were doing. It's where I learned one of the contractors was a competitive badminton player!

Lunchtime at work is a unique opportunity. It is where deals can be made, issues clarified, or, often, in my case, friends made.

CHAPTER 3

SOULS IN SOLES

"I just felt like running."

–Forrest Gump

Runners. Either a person's reaction is to groan or excitedly say, "Yes! Finally!" I am admittedly the butt of the joke: "How do you know there is a runner in the room? ... They tell you!"

My twenties and thirties saw me frequently start, stop, or attempt a running routine. Invariably, I would quit running due to injury or being overwhelmed by my schedule, convinced I would never join the ranks of my family.

My parents ran when I was young, and my uncles and older cousins ran at that time, too, and continued to run as I grew older. Then my younger brother and cousins, who were closer to my age, also began running. The natural pressure was on me to join this familial collective.

It wasn't until two significant moments in my life that it finally fell into place for me. In late 2008 and early 2009, the economy went into a recession. Layoffs were brutal.

Starbucks was no different from other corporations. No one was immune to the bleak economy. While I retained my job, the instability, strain, and near chaos of how to do twice as much work with half as many people created a stressful work environment.

When under a great deal of stress, my stomach tightens and knots. I can't eat. Or more accurately, I eat very little. By the way, I do **not** endorse or recommend this as a weight loss solution. Regardless, during that time, I lost about fifteen pounds.

With the weight loss, I reasoned that I could maintain it and try running as a form of stress management. I figured a small, manageable distance, such as three to five miles a few times per week, was reasonable to maintain. Those first weeks running were neither swift nor as easy as I imagined in my Walter Mitty mind.

Then, as I was surely starting to resemble Phoebe from *Friends* running down the street, an article on running form caught my eye. In my most recent copy of *Women's Health* magazine, an article detailed how to coordinate breath with gait. Specifically, how to nose breathe and not mouth breathe while running.

After reading the article, it took me one or two attempts, and it all clicked into place. I maintained a smooth and steady pace.

Most importantly, I found an outlet to deal with the stress in a healthy and productive manner. Therefore, I was adamant that I would only run for stress relief and management.

After several months of this new style of running, a few friends needled, urged, and insisted I start racing. A full marathon seemed daunting. Plus, I watched my dad burn out running 26.2 miles. The half-marathon option seemed more plausible.

In early 2010, a friend offered to help me build a training plan to run a half-marathon, complete with my day off being Fridays, so I could still go to Happy Hour! Priorities! It was a twelve-week plan that would steadily guide me to the first weekend in May. He warned me, "Heather, once you cross that finish line, something will change inside of you." That was all he said.

Exactly as my friend promised, when I passed that final solid white line, with the screaming crowds, the finishing medals glinting in the sunlight in Vancouver, British Columbia, and a respectable time of two hours and ten minutes, I was hooked!

I competed in two additional races that year. My newfound passion solidified and ensconced me into a new club filled with supportive, understanding, and excited members. I had found my people. I was happy, healthy, and discovering this previously unknown side of me—*a half-marathon runner.*

★ ★ ★

I always learn something new about myself when I decide to train for and run a half-marathon. What the lesson is varies for me with each training run.

I have learned there were days when my body was tired and did not want to run, yet after about a half mile, I was grateful I went. On the converse, there were days when I knew it was a bad idea to run for fear of injury. I accepted that wisdom intervened in those moments.

According to a Gitnux report[4] from a compilation of sources, half-marathons are comprised of 61% women with an average age of 39 years old. Runners invest an average of $120 per pair of shoes, with Nike being the most popular brand at 30% of all shoes. I am not a Nike shoe wearer. I was loyal to New Balance for a long time and then recently joined the Hoka movement.

The average race registration fee in the United States costs between $60 and $80. I agree with this average. I generally try to identify my race selections to get the early bird pricing.

Like the training plan my friend built, the average runner trains for twelve to fourteen weeks ahead of the race. While I have squeaked out an eight-week plan, it is neither ideal nor suggested for anyone new to half-marathon racing.

In none of these statistics did the data capture my *secret* on the night before the race—a single glass of Merlot during the carb (carbohydrate) load meal. There are specific wineries that I consider produce a "race worthy" Merlot. Those I will *not* disclose!

The carb load meal is a time-honored tradition. Plenty of data around dietary approaches to pre-race and race-day sustenance exists. I have learned that it is a smart idea to test the pre-race and race-day meals during one of the long run training weeks.

---

[4] "Be Ahead of the Market with Reliable Data," Gitnux Market Data: Statistics & Reports, accessed May 26, 2025, https://gitnux.org/half-marathon-statistics/.

The carb load pre-race meal tradition is generally one of community and togetherness that cannot be underestimated. It's a time to celebrate all the training (or not). To laugh, share, relax, and prepare for the big moment.

I was unsuccessful in locating sufficient data on how this meal in a community setting (more than one person) helps the runner's performance on race day, but I believe it does.

Much like my lunches, that sense of connection is invaluable when trying to do one's best for 13.1 miles (or 21.1 kilometers). With limited data on community benefits, I can only provide what I have observed.

Some races I have run offer a communal pre-race meal for all distances, including 10K, Half, and Full Marathons. Usually, it's some form of pasta dinner, balanced with salad and a dinner roll.

What I have witnessed at these meals is the dynamics between the racer and their support crew, which is often friends or family cheering from the sidelines. Sometimes, the racer was completely disengaged in conversation, and other times, they were indeed the life of the party. The support crew could often be quiet, a bit hesitant, and uncertain, trying to ensure that all details were covered and met.

Conversations floated around the room or hall with snippets of "Oh man, that was the worst race I ever ran!" or "Yes, Cathy was so patient and helpful when I hurt my ankle and hobbled to her at mile 11." The race-day emotions of excitement and anticipation were palpable.

As the racers and crew left the dining hall, I was certain I would not recognize either side when I raced the next day. A transformation occurs overnight: makeup is washed off, hair is let down, faces are shaven or unshaven, and that cup of coffee that wasn't drunk fast enough.

Since the event quickly grew from a hundred or so people eating in the same dining area to thousands of bodies, recognizing someone from the previous evening became nearly impossible.

My lunches in this section were with female runners who are anything but average, like the half-marathon statistics. While I had lunch with each of these women separately, I could easily see all of us together at a pre-race carb-loading meal. These women would instantly bond and immediately share their stories and journeys. The communal effect is instantaneous.

These women all have varying degrees of race experience and distance. Yet, in our separate lunches and beyond, I have learned much about running. Their range of miles spanned from 5Ks (3.1 miles) to Ultra Marathons (greater than thirty-one miles) and Iron Man races.

Running BFF Lunch

Anthea is one of my oldest and dearest friends from Starbucks. We knew each other nearly the entire time I worked there (save two weeks). She was on leave when I started. I sat in her cubicle, and I remember hearing about what a great person and teammate she was. I knew I had to meet this person whose work life I had inadvertently invaded.

We met and became fast friends. Eventually, through some cubicle location moves, we even became office roommates, shoehorned into a small office. We made it work.

The office was a tight fit for what we did—we had lots of mugs and tumbler samples. We HAD to get along, or ceramic mugs were going to be flying through short distances.

In addition to sharing an office, Anthea and I worked on the same team. I was the sourcing development for her sourcing operations. Then, in later years, we worked on adjoining supply chain teams and were completely independent and not affiliated.

Through it all, we determined how to balance our personal and professional lives to make it all work. It wasn't easy, yet it was beyond worth it.

In both our work and personal lives, we shared big moments and little moments. Laughter, tears, frustrations, anger, certainty, instability, too many drinks, not enough drinks, late nights, and early mornings. Her incredible cooking, my eating her cooking, traveling for races, racing in the same town, pain in the ass co-workers, pain in the ass suppliers, unreasonable deadlines, making those deadlines and feeling like we conquered the world, pushing each other, listening to each other, sharing, caring, and finding comfort in our friendship.

Twelve years might not seem like a long time to some people for a friendship duration, but it is a lifetime to me. I am beyond blessed to know Anthea and call her my friend.

She left Starbucks almost five years before my Coffee Break. One of my greatest honors was reciting a poem I wrote for her on her last day. I physically shook badly, and yet, my voice never wavered. I spoke from my heart and told what I knew to be true about my friend and coworker.

After her departure, I missed her desperately. I yearned for the ability to climb five flights of stairs to the ninth floor to bitch, complain, worry, share joys, or share accomplishments. There was a solace in my heart in knowing she was in the building that gave me deep comfort and true happiness. Then it was gone.

As we sat down at the high-top table for our lunch, I asked, "How is the new gig going?"

She smiled and then sighed, "As well as can be expected." Then, looking me dead in the eye, she asked, "How is the Coffee Break going?"

At that point, I was about three months in with some travel already under my belt. I shared the excitement of my music cities trip. "I started in Memphis, as one should. Then on to Muscle Shoals, Alabama. Next, I went to Nashville. From there, I went to New Orleans. And finally, I stopped in Austin, Texas."

Naturally, as we always do, the conversation turned to our same age/same grade kids. We compared the details of all the "last moments" we were participating in since our oldest children were seniors in high school: the last game or event, the last first day of school, etc.

Then, she got a gleam in her eye. "Speaking of your time in New Orleans, what would you think if we ran the New Orleans Rock and Roll Half Marathon in February? Remember the fun we had running the BMO Vancouver (British Columbia) Half Marathon last year? I think we should travel again."

It was my turn to grin. There wasn't a bit of hesitation in my mind. We'd tested our friendship the previous year in Canada by sharing a hotel room and spending the weekend together.

I was certain we would again have a great time. I thought, *And escape the misery of Seattle winters?* "I'm pretty sure I can make it happen." This was a splendid idea!

While I am generally a lone wolf when I run, Anthea is one of the few people I have trained with a handful of times. We don't run at the same pace, and yet, as our friendship attests, that doesn't matter. The half-marathons we have participated in have been both local to the Seattle area and our favorite: destination races.

In February 2019, when Seattle was being threatened with a blanket of historical snow, Anthea and I snuck out of the dreary winter and landed in the welcoming, colorful city of New Orleans, Louisiana. Having previously been there in the fall, I felt the familiarity of family and fun.

One thing about Anthea is that if you are friends with her, it is very likely you aren't alone. True to form, three of Anthea's friends joined us in New Orleans. The five of us had a blast!

Somehow, they all twisted my arm into running a "remix," which I learned was two races in one weekend. We ran the 5K on Saturday and the half-marathon on Sunday! That was a first for me.

That weekend, and especially at the pre-race carb meal, we shared stories, tales, and memories of races from the past—the times when it was hotter than Hades or colder than a snowman.

I looked around the table at the four expectant faces. "My memorable race to share was the year of the soaking wet Seattle Half Marathon. (This race was run the Sunday after Thanksgiving.) That particular year, a rainstorm hit *during* the race. Despite my Gore-Tex rain gear, I was absolutely soaked to the bone. Eventually, people were skirting around large puddles on the roads. Cold, wet, and frustrated, I decided to plow literally *through* the puddles. I wanted to be done. One such puddle shocked me when it went up to my mid-calf. Soon after that, the cruel, slight rise at the end was a welcome sight."

Groans of knowing that final part passed through the group. "I blew into the stadium grouchier than I had ever been. And yet … Yep, I couldn't wait for my next race!" Everyone laughed and then shared their "worst race ever stories."

Our group traveled well together, eating and drinking, laughing, sharing, and supporting. We vowed to do it again somewhere else. Unfortunately, the one story none of us had ever experienced that surprised us all was that COVID shut down races for the foreseeable future.

When I recall this lunch, I can only be submerged in gratitude and wholeness. We should all be as fortunate as I am to have a friend in this world like Anthea. My heart misses our daily interactions, yet I feel exceptionally full knowing we are friends.

Sun Devil Runner Lunch

Tara and I met through the Starbucks Running Club. Even though we never ran together, her intention to run for reasons beyond the self is an inspiration for running and general fitness.

She confidently strode into the restaurant with a large grin on her face. Dressed in her signature goldish yellow with hints of maroon, I smiled to myself. She was forever a representation of the Arizona State Sun Devils.

My lunch with her was highly anticipated because I was excited to discuss her most recent race. Nearly a day and a half before we sat down for Thai food, Tara had run the highly revered Marine Corps Marathon in Washington, DC. Decades before, my dad had run this same race.

She made me envious with how great she looked after having run 26.2 miles, roughly forty-eight hours before our lunch. She appeared refreshed, with her outfit smartly put together.

When I noticed her navigating easily through the restaurant to our booth seating, my mouth hung wide open. *How does she look this good this quickly after a marathon?*

I am not always a poster child for "reasons to run" after completing a half-marathon. Often, my IT band tightens up on one or both sides of my thighs. (The IT band, or iliotibial band, is the tendon outside the leg that goes from the top of the pelvis down to the knee.)

When that occurs, it is all I can do to push through the discomfort and finish. Never mind that all the while I am sweating profusely, breathing heavily, and grinning some likely maniacal smile.

I soon learned that by her standards, she wasn't entirely ready for this race. In my opinion, she had a very respectable finishing time of 4:38:37. Far from her personal best or even what she hoped to achieve, she smiled and commented, "Heather, some races you run for fun, not for time." Maybe someday I will learn to relax and enjoy the race, rather than worrying about the time.

Tara's military support is not limited to the Marines. As a proud Arizona State Sun Devil, Tara is active with the Pat Tillman Foundation. Pat Tillman was an American football player who donned the number 42 to play as a linebacker for the Arizona State Sun Devils in the mid-1990s.

In 1998, he didn't venture too far away from college to begin his NFL career as a safety for the Arizona Cardinals. In the aftermath of the 9/11 attacks, Tillman elected to leave his NFL career behind and enlisted in the U.S. Army. His life was cut short when he died in the line of duty on April 22, 2004.

The Sun Devil community, in concert with the Pat Tillman Foundation, hosts Pat's Run in Tempe, Arizona, each April. Pat's Run consists of covering 4.2 miles (or 0.42 miles for the little ones) either walking or running.

Proceeds go to support the Pat Tillman Foundation, supporting the Tillman Scholar Program, which is a selective community of military service members, veterans, and military spouses. These scholars exhibit a willingness to demonstrate leadership while addressing challenges across a multitude of platforms, ranging from local to global scale.

Even though she lives far away from Arizona, Tara is highly active with the Alumni Association. She has helped to host remote runs for those who can't make it to Tempe, Arizona, in April. I was able to participate in 2016, when she co-hosted the race in Tacoma, Washington, with the Starbucks Running Club and the Starbucks Armed Forces Network. She and I were both highly active participants in the latter group.

Tara left Starbucks two years before I started my Coffee Break. We took this opportunity to connect over our shared experience of living in the same general area. She bought a home along a greenbelt not far from where I lived. My head started to feel dizzy as I listened to her roll through all her activities outside of work and running. Travel and supporting the arts were two of her big highlights.

She never ceases to amaze me with her energy. My only guess is that somehow she has more than 24 hours like the rest of us. Yet, she finds time to pause, enjoy moments with a glass of wine, a quiet evening on her back deck, or meeting a friend for lunch at a local eatery.

Mirror Reflection Lunch

When I run in my neighborhood, I sometimes wonder about the people who live in certain houses. I contemplate how many people live there, or what they are making for Sunday breakfast, or if they are happy with their job or, or …

I did mention that I am not a fast runner, right? Time is often on my side while passing homes. It wasn't until we were formally introduced that I learned I had always run past Jolene's home.

Jolene was a person whom I would see at functions, yet I never had one-on-one time with her. Therefore, it was an absolute pleasure to sit across from her. This was an opportunity to learn more about her without the distractions of a party or function setting.

On a brisk and cold day in the winter, we met at a local restaurant. As she shared her stories, interests, and hobbies, I swore I was looking into a mirror reflection. I saw her eyes light up as mine did when she talked about reading. I can talk for hours about reading alone!

A passion for traveling is also a shared interest between us. Pair with that, as you would in respect to wines, a trip to wine country to enjoy the shades of red within a glass as well as the notes of spice or cocoa. We agreed that living on the West Coast allows for some great trips to amazing wineries.

She doesn't only travel for good wine. I could almost hear the live music she spoke of when she talked about traveling to see a concert. She leaned forward in her seat, wanting to hear about my music trip to six different U.S. music cities. Happily, I shared my travel stories.

We chuckled as we realized that both of us had returned from quick trips to warmer locales. Both of us also travel to escape the cold, gray, and bleak weather that frequently occurs in our part of the Pacific Northwest.

While it is scenic and green year-round with its evergreen trees and mountains, there comes a time in the winter when the gray days become cumbersome, and I experience a form of claustrophobia due to a lack of direct sunshine. Travel of some sort is how many of us cope.

As I explained at the beginning of this chapter, it is easy to know when there is a runner in the room—they tell you! Running is the first hobby that connected Jolene and me. Naturally, it was great fun to talk running with her during our lunch.

Even though she and I have never trained or raced together, periodically we would share previous races we have run. Her voice became excited, telling me how she and her girlfriends will be running the Vacation Races Zion National Park Half Marathon.

I gasped, "I ran that half-marathon last year!"

She laughed and said, "Oh yes, I know you did."

I couldn't tell her quickly enough about how beautiful the race was! The shades of reds, oranges, and deep browns streaking across the land. With Zion, the course is often changed. I ran the version that was on top of a plateau that started at a 5,580-foot elevation with a gain of 686 feet. The peaks of the nearby mountains provided humble moments of feeling insignificant in this large world.

As it was for me, this would be her first trip to Zion National Park. She is in for a treat! Beyond the race, the national park is beautiful, majestic, and breathtaking. I was very excited for her. She and her girlfriends will have a fabulous time.

Jolene participates in the Tough Mudder challenges. This awed me, and I wanted to hear more from her perspective. It looks like a great time and personally rewarding, yet I know my propensity for injury. When I see those races, I see a broken ankle in my always accident-prone future.

She shared, "The Tough Mudder is fun because I get completely muddy and push my body to limits I didn't know were possible." Listening to Jolene and others tell their stories is the closest I will ever get. Much respect!

Our work was where we diverged into different paths. Jolene is self-employed with a fascinating job as a home stager. She works with a couple of local realtors to help "stage" furniture in homes to sell.

She confidently said, "I have certain pieces of furniture I rent or use to set a room with a homey feeling." It sounded like a great part-time job that allows her to work as many or as few hours as her schedule can handle.

Toward the end of our lunch, our paths intersected again. For some time, I have been curious about Jolene's writing career. I knew through our mutual friends that she was a published author.

Prior to our lunch, I wanted to learn more about the handful of books she had written. I timidly said to her, "Jolene, despite my best attempts to research, I have come up short when I tried to find your books."

She smiled widely, with that familiar confidence. "I write under the pen name of 'Alex Strong'; my books are in the romance genre."

I laughed, feeling less foolish, "Aha! You are a wise woman to use a pen name!" While romance is not normally the genre that I read—I'm still getting through all the musician biographies—one of these days, I will read one of her books.

Run for a Cause Lunch

Jodi and I met for lunch on an uncharacteristically warm spring day in the Pacific Northwest. The area had been hitting record-high early springtime temperatures for a few days. The warmer temperatures and sunshine naturally put both of us in wonderful moods with the renewed energy, like a runner poking out of the dark woods knows.

Lunch with Jodi was a face-to-face moment to hear about her running efforts and endeavors, uninterrupted, other than the waitstaff asking for our food order. She amazes me with all the races and destinations where she has crossed a finish line, including Boston, Paris, and London. This was my time to learn more.

We were introduced through mutual friends. Immediately, in my mind, she was the "mighty marathoner." I always enjoyed seeing Jodi at functions or a friend's house. Her laugh is jovial and one that makes you comfortably join in. Of course, at these parties, all the runners talk shop as the others (non-runners) naturally back away. We share a knowing giggle, as we are used to it.

Generally, at these parties, four or five runners are comparing recent running stories and moments. Regardless of our alienation from the rest of the party, it is evident that we support each other. Whether it is running to achieve a personal record (PR), a qualifying time (QT), or to make a difference supporting a charity, the collective group experiences those moments and that understanding.

During our lunch, I shared with Jodi, "Running has given to me, created me, and humbled me. I may not put in the miles like you do, yet I still put in miles. Each one means something." She nodded with a knowing look. I continued, "Even the seemingly routine training runs past your house teach me a lesson each time."

I asked Jodi to rehash the various marathons in different locations. Since I come from a family of runners, I knew the prestige and honor that came with attempting to qualify for the Boston Marathon. We discussed her working to qualify for Boston. Her voice resolute, "The qualifying times are fast! Even though they start to decrease, your age starts to increase. It doesn't make it easy. And yet, I was successful and qualified!" I was elated for her!

With little irony, I shared that I lived vicariously through her miles. Currently, I have no interest in running full marathons, though some cities that offer only full marathons make it tempting to reconsider my stance. *Maybe Chicago someday, Jodi. Maybe.*

There are numerous half-marathon races where I have seen someone pushing a loved one for 13.1 or 26.2 miles—or at least shared duty. Witnessing a person run while pushing a wheel-chair or similar device is humbling.

However, it is the determination and sense of purpose in both participants' eyes that always makes me slow my pace a little. I am honored to be part of their moment, if only for a few steps.

Jodi often runs with a higher purpose. I wanted to learn more about this as we ate lunch. "Tell me about how all the training and racing miles you put in are not simply for yourself."

As the sun filters in through the windows, she sits up taller and shares, "I am an avid runner for awareness and fundraising for the United Cerebral Palsy Foundation. Specifically, a group known as Micah's Miles." (Or as I always remember, Micah Smiles: www.micahsmiles.org.) Every picture on the website is of an endearing young boy with a beautiful smile (so it makes it easy to remember the website name).

"Micah is my nephew," she tells me. With that familiar determination of someone pushing a wheelchair, she reflected on the numerous marathons that she and her family have run, pushing him across finish lines. They agree to share the miles, alternating who pushes Micah and who paces with the team.

With a flutter in my heart, I thought to myself what a wondrous moment it must be to work together as a family unit, recalling the memories of the races when I saw people pushing young children and adults, each runner looking forward with more than the finish line in their sights.

Running is a deeply personal journey. To the spectator world, it appears to be about physical fitness and feats. Yet, I know, and I know Jodi would agree, it is so much more. You learn what you are made of, or what you can endure, and what you can push aside to get to where you need to be.

As we finished lunch, I thought to myself, *My hope for other people is that they have a person like Jodi in their life.* Someone whom you secretly say, "Yes, she's here!" because you know you are going to have a great evening at a party. Someone whose presence and purpose make you fortunate to know them.

There is a saying among runners: "I run for those who are no longer here or who cannot."

Sometimes, even when a person cannot run with their legs, another human being will find a way to help get them across the finish line. Someday, I am certain that I will humbly see Jodi and Micah at the finish line.

The Wrap-Up

My favorite race to run is the North Olympic Discovery (Half) Marathon. This point-to-point race goes from Sequim (pronounced squim) to Port Angeles. It is on the picturesque North Olympic Discovery Trail on the Olympic Peninsula.

There is a humorous tongue-in-cheek joke that there are more volunteers than runners. Given how smoothly both the half and full marathons are executed year after year, it almost seems like the truth.

Adequately equipped with water stations that compete for the best station, each has a different theme. I have run past "The Avengers" water stop, "The Port Angeles Marching Band," or a Seattle sports-themed water stop with plenty of Skittles and blue and green decorations.

There is a large amount of participation from people in the local community. I appreciate hearing one of the local high school marching bands play "The Star-Spangled Banner" prior to the start of the race, seeing ham-radio operators ready to offer a hand, and local artists designing the finishing medals. The carb-load pasta dinner hosted by the Lions Club is a big highlight for me.

Participation aside, the racecourse is breathtaking. I ran on the paved path in a grove of mature cedar trees and other evergreens. What race in the Pacific Northwest is complete without some challenging hills? My favorite part of the course is around mile nine. Suddenly, I pop out of the forest and gasp when I see the Strait of Juan de Fuca—the cool blue water, the glimpses of snow-capped mountains, and the evergreen trees towering above the skyline. It gets me every time.

The remainder of the race is along the Strait; on clear days, it isn't hard to see the Canadian border. On windy days, it's difficult to push ahead while fighting gusts. It isn't long before the finish line is visible. It seems so close, and yet, it is deceptively still another two and a half miles away.

One of the most memorable signs I see at almost every one of the twenty-seven half-marathons I have run is "Go Random Stranger!" It always makes me laugh.

The roar of the crowd lifts my spirits to get me to that final point one mile. It is at that moment that I am a part of someone's family, friend group, or work colleague. It doesn't matter that I will never know their names, nor they mine. What matters is that they are celebrating my accomplishment with me, for me.

It chokes me up.

During the lunches I had in this chapter, we talked about our favorite races and finish lines. Regardless of the story, we agree that there is truth to the saying, "It's not how I finish, it is that I had the courage to begin."

CHAPTER 4

ALL BECAUSE OF KETCHUP

*"Better to see something once than hear about
it a thousand times."*

—Asian Proverb

When I was young, my dad's company allowed him to save his vacation time and use several weeks all at once. He and my mom dreamed of traveling across the United States to visit national parks, family, tourist attractions, etc. Three times over the course of seven years, my parents, brother, and I traveled from Pennsylvania to various destinations in the Midwest, the West, and parts of Canada.

Depending on the point of view, our form of travel either appeared rather primitive or somewhat commonplace. The first year, we ventured west in the newest vehicular invention: the introduction of the all-American classic modern vehicle, the minivan.

Being a one-income family, this meant that we traveled in a five-passenger, five-speed red Dodge Caravan. (Do they even make five-passenger minivans now, much less a five-speed?)

Knowing very little about traveling and packing requirements for five weeks, my dad decided to build a travel trailer to tow behind the minivan. No, not to sleep in. That honor was reserved for our REI four-person, stack-'em-like-cord-wood tent.

This trailer was designed to haul extra luggage, house the camping stove, cooking equipment, cooler, and any other incidentals we thought we might not be able to live without.

I would watch thirty-foot crystal-white RVs, tan pop-up campers, or military gray fifth-wheel configurations drive past us and wish for a "real bed." Our setup became not-so-bad when we stopped at a rest area and witnessed what could have been our fate had we not had the utility trailer.

A family was also putting in thousands of miles to travel across the U.S. in their minivan, except they had no trailer. Everything, plus possibly the kitchen sink, was stuffed, crammed, and shoved into the back of the van. Fortunately for this family, this was in the days before cell phones could record what came next.

The meltdown.

It was clear from the volume across the parking lot that the family members were on each other's very last nerve. Something of urgent importance, like a napkin, was buried at the bottom of the pile in the back of the van.

It's easy to picture what came next. The dad tried to unpack layer by layer. Realizing he was neither a brick mason nor a military loadmaster, items shifted and began to tumble onto the parking lot.

The mom was refereeing the two brats who were swinging at each other, and all the while, she was coaching, barking orders at her husband as if she had recently retired from a drill sergeant career.

It was a sight to behold and hear. The sweat of that hot day and this family meltdown still trickles down my back.

It was difficult to avert our eyes from the train wreck on the macadam. In that moment, we all felt a sigh of relief that my dad had the foresight to assemble something to ease the travel burden.

Not that we weren't without our own meltdown. I was the definite catalyst that triggered the domino effect. It is a general wonder I am not still sitting at a rest stop on I-90, hoping to be adopted into some family.

All over ketchup.

We pulled into a rest stop to eat breakfast, which was our long travel-day custom: rise early to pack up the tent, sleeping bags, and rolls, pound out a few hours on the interstate, and dine on the morning meal.

On the menu that day (as most days) were egg sandwiches with ketchup. My turn was first to get the sandwich bread and put some ketchup on the slices. Thinking I was a genius, I slammed a dollop of Heinz goodness (as a Pennsylvania family, Heinz is a state requirement) on my slices of wheat bread, smeared them together, and waited for my egg. Easy enough, right?

Wrong. One of my parents (I will protect the innocent party) told me to use a butter knife. I, being the pre-teen agreeable child, said in a rather smug tone, "That's not necessary; I have it handled."

My parent turned a deeper shade of red than the color of ketchup could ever be. This ignited a massive explosion of irritation, anger, and frustration. Soon enough, we were all at each other's throats for every little grievance or perceived wrongdoing since the dawn of time.

We quickly became the sideshow spectacle as families sat in their RVs, tsking us for being ridiculous and pitiful. I'm happy to report that I was permitted to stay with my family for the remainder of that trip with little to no incidents.

Despite the harrowing moments tent-camping across the United States as an adolescent, there were incredible occasions viewing the Grand Canyon, feeling like an ant in the Redwood Forest, looking out the window with my jaw dropping in the Grand Tetons, and lying beneath a star-filled sky in the South Dakota Badlands. All these experiences fostered and developed my love for traveling and sightseeing.

My lunch guests in this chapter all have an affinity for travel. Therefore, talking about our experiences, including our worst and best travel stories, was a great way to spend our respective lunches.

French Quarter Lunch

Having lunch in the French Quarter of New Orleans, Louisiana, with Patricia was a definite travel highlight. One barely needs to close their eyes to instantly imagine the bright yellows, greens, pinks, purples, and blues that decorate New Orleans, even without having ever been there.

However, I highly encourage the trip! The colors portray the exciting energy that is quickly complemented by a loud brass band parade performing in a square. This is a way of life, family, and friendship for the people of New Orleans.

I have known Patricia for the better part of twelve years. We met through our mutual friend Dave when she briefly lived in Seattle. The friendship endured even as she moved to different cities, always returning for visits and rekindling the days gone by.

She and her partner were living in New Orleans when I was there. I was thrilled that it worked out for us to have lunch and spend some time catching up. Coordinating schedules for all my lunches was daunting! Add in the complexity of visiting a different city, and it became even more tricky.

An inviting and stately, bold red brick-cased building with contrasting black wrought iron railing on the second story welcomed me to dine. We met for lunch in the French Quarter at a lovely restaurant called Muriel's on the northern corner of Jackson Square.

Like all the architecture in New Orleans, Muriel's restaurant was a marvelous building rich with history. New Orleans structures contain infinite stories, lore, and a touch of the paranormal.

Our conversation naturally began by catching up on our mutual friends from the Seattle area. We share some very dear friends, a few of whom made it into this book! There was a palpable moment at lunch when we both felt blessed to be able to talk about everyone. We are most fortunate.

Patricia has a beautiful laugh that instantly transports us back to our memories of Washington. Between gasps of laughter and near tears, she started with, "Do you remember that time at the Halloween party when we …?"

Trying my best not to wet my shorts, I chimed in, "Or that time when that girl almost passed out on our table at the Honky-Tonk bar?"

Our stories never get old, and we never tire of retelling them to any soul who is lucky enough to be nearby.

We spent part of our lunch talking about a New Orleans event I have yet to attend—Jazz Fest. For the unindoctrinated, it is a huge music festival where countless musicians perform. Many of them are my favorites!

Generally, this is held for two full weekends at the end of April and the beginning of May. I do need to attend. If I've heard it once, I've heard it a hundred times. Regardless of who the person is, if they know that I am a music fan, they end their conversation with a simple, *You must attend Jazz Fest!*

New Orleans has a feeling of being one of the most all-encompassing artistically creative hubs in the United States. Patricia and I also spent our time comparing notes as writers and artists. Passion oozed, excitement filled our voices, and creativity swirled in the air. It felt very New Orleans-like to sit down to a meal and talk about our books, our writing, and our respective creative processes.

What lunch is complete without dessert? We left Muriel's and made our way to The Palace for bananas Foster and coffee. While the restaurant offers a menu of meals, as I walked in, I smelled the scent of sugar, cinnamon, butter, bananas, and a touch of rum constantly wafting around the grand room.

Bananas Foster at The Palace was theatrical and tantalizing. The server stopped tableside with a silvery service cart that had a gas burner in the center. Each step was purposeful, almost delayed, causing more anticipation for the grand event: flambé.

The scaling blue and yellow flames from the rum additive are supposed to rise dramatically atop the bananas, butter, and brown sugar mixture. Sadly, our batch was not a flaming ball of fire, which sometimes happens—it was extraordinary, nonetheless. We weren't disappointed because the dessert was utterly delicious. I can almost still taste it as I recall the moment.

After lunch and our bananas Foster dessert, Patricia and her partner gave me a walking local's tour. It was a splendid September day! The sky was that shade of azure blue that contrasted with the colorful building rooflines. The temperatures were in the upper 70s, and it was an unusually low-humidity day. My mind spun from seeing so many different historically and literarily significant sights.

At one point, we stopped in front of a seemingly benign white building. Patricia's partner turned to me, then looked back at the building. He declared, "This is the world-famous 'House of the Rising Sun.'"

I couldn't hold back and exclaimed, "No way!"

As I took a double take, it was still so boring and lacked description. Then I realized that sometimes songs build much more imagery in our minds than the reality would bear.

Patricia's partner had a wealth of knowledge about the city. He knew where William Faulkner penned certain books. I saw the cathedral where Patricia's partner's parents were married. I also saw the hospital where his life started.

As we walked, I learned and saw a very different side of New Orleans, one that no tour book or tour group would ever adequately capture.

My private local's tour walked through Antoine's. This is the restaurant where the crowned Mardi Gras king and queen cut the ceremonial cake to begin the official festivities.

While listening to the two of them chatter on, I was transformed into a city full of deep and wonderful history, not the superficial drinking town many see or sadly only experience. Beneath the colors was a world of family, connection, and heritage.

Busy Traveler Lunch

There are some people in my life who absolutely awe me. People who remember seemingly small details or even impactful events from my life: one of those individuals is Matthew.

Matthew and I know each other from our time working at Starbucks. I can't recall the moment I met him; I can say he has been one of the best people I've been with at Happy Hour.

For us to have lunch together almost felt a bit irreverent, except that occasionally we did have lunch in the corporate building. Mostly, though, Matthew and I were Happy Hour pals.

In all our time knowing each other, Matthew and I have criss-crossed our professional paths in what I can only describe as shooting stars across the same sky. While we both began in Supply Chain, we have never worked on the same team or directly supported each other.

Yet, our larger teams or groups interacted. If he had a question or needed a favor, I was among the first for him to Instant Message, and vice versa. Halfway through my career, I moved to IT, and our relationship continued. We both knew that the other would find the answer if one wasn't readily available. It's good to have a working relationship like that.

What I value more is our friendship. Thus, our countless Happy Hour excursions. Primarily, we used to haunt a bar that we affectionately called "Starbucks North."

There was a core group of friends/coworkers that I could count on seeing on Fridays. Matthew always laughed at my frantic scramble to make my train south. Sometimes, he would clear a path or arrange a driver for me to stay a little longer. It's good to have a buddy like that.

Matthew has always made me feel appreciated. He remembers moments my kids or I have experienced. He makes it a point to ask about my family whenever I see him. He is continuously genuine and real.

Matthew wholeheartedly supported my decision to take a Coffee Break. He also had the opportunity to take one for six months. He traveled and rested. It made a huge impact on his life.

Occasionally, he checked on me to see how my Coffee Break was going. I greatly appreciated it. I wondered if I would lose track of some friends while I was on break, but not Matthew. Given both mine and Matthew's travels, it took us a while to coordinate schedules for lunch, but it was well worth the wait.

We met at a great little Mexican restaurant in a fantastic part of Seattle. I think we both felt at ease in that area. There was something about the eclectic and genuine character of the location that made us both comfortable.

He said one of the best statements when we sat down, "Okay, I want to hear all about your break, the high points *and* the low points."

Did I mention he was sincere? I had to think for a few moments. After almost eleven months, what were my high points? What were my low points?

It didn't take long to assemble my list. We were off and running with our conversation. I highlighted and went into depth on each angle. It was great fun to reflect with him. His eyes were always watching for my body language to emphasize an emotion.

We discussed recent happenings at Starbucks—who was hired, who left, and how layoffs affected groups or mutual friends. He and I became quiet, sharing a mutual moment of sorrow, honoring those who lost their jobs.

After the somber pause, his quip was right on time. "Of course, you know the inevitable. Our team moved floors, *again*." I laughed out loud, appreciating Matthew's gifts of wit and sarcasm.

While we were catching up on the general state of business, it felt like a different universe at times. Then he would mention someone, and it felt like I was back in the building. How is it that everything in a relationship can change and yet nothing can change? I guess that's how it is when you have been friends for a long time.

If there is one thing that I love to listen to when I connect with Matthew, it's his travels. He is a world traveler or a chronic United States traveler. I am certain it would come as no surprise that he has friends around the globe. He constantly gets a local's tour and treatment when he travels.

While I only know a small handful of his mates, I envision that, much like me, his larger friend network feels appreciated and valued when he visits. I attribute this camaraderie to his keen and personal memory.

I have seen firsthand that he treats others the same as he treats me; he listens, he remembers, he's compassionate. I think that speaks volumes about his character. I am fortunate to know him.

As I neared my potential return to work, there was a sense of trepidation and a bit of anxiety. He laughed when I said, "My big worry is that I will forget people's names!" He knows that is important to me.

He was honest too. "It's going to take a bit of time to adjust back into the corporate world."

I did not take his advice lightly. I knew he was perfectly correct. This would be an adjustment physically, mentally, and even emotionally. I was grateful to have Matthew in my support corner to help with the reentry.

Libra Lunch

After the always comforting hugs, Becky and I sat down at our table in the quaint restaurant that was an old home with red siding. She is almost my twin, as I am only three days older than she is. We met when our daughters were in kindergarten together.

Immediately, we began talking about our recent travels. She frequently travels for work, both domestically and internationally. We discussed the places we've seen and the experiences we've had. I filled her in on my eleven-day music city trip.

"Becky, I am still trying to figure out how I can get a trip to Savannah, Georgia, scheduled with you. It is one of my favorite cities; I would love to have you as a travel companion to such a beautiful place. I can't believe you've never been there," I exclaimed.

She laughed, sighed, and said, "I know. It's this job of mine that keeps me traveling." She works on filming and producing training and instructional videos for a gaming company.

It wasn't until I had my lunch with her that I realized how similar our early years were. Funny how with kids and life today, that conversation never happened. We've even talked about our teenage years, yet never touched on those early years. I am pleased we finally did.

I was in awe, thinking about how she and I probably listened to some of the same music at the same time. Was she playing a Harry Chapin record on an April day in the early '80s? Was she listening to and twirling around her living room on a cold January day to Donna Summer like I was? Did her dad sit in the living room with the baby poop green 1970s furniture with her and play Jim Croce, The Mamas and the Papas, or Peter, Paul, and Mary like my dad did? We would name musician after musician from the 1960s and 1970s, and yes, the other listened to that music. It quickly became a fun game.

Somewhere in our early teens, our music choices changed. I took the more rock and heavy metal path; she went on to the more pop and dance route. Our differences in music tastes today are still as far apart, yet that doesn't prevent us from talking about music.

That's what I love about music. Even with our differences, we are all still alike. Something moves us, something stirs us. While it might sound different, the beat speaks to each of us.

Becky and I talked about our extended families and her previous and recent experiences with family members who have dementia. I listened and then I hesitantly asked, "Have you ever heard about the documentary *Alive Inside*?"

Quizzically, she looked at me and responded, "No, I haven't."

I gently smiled and cleared my throat a little, "It is worth the box of tissues to watch."

The documentary is a fascinating look at a new trend in the treatment of dementia and Alzheimer's patients. The medicine?

Music. The video showed patients in memory care facilities wearing headphones on their ears. This shocked me. I figured there would be some fussing or rejection on the patient's part. Those moments may have occurred and were on the cutting room floor.

The headphones began to play music that the patients may have heard when they were teenagers or in their early twenties. There were patients who, day after day, would sit in a chair with their heads nearly touching the table. People who were barely responsive, not knowing the family member who came to visit. As soon as the headphones were placed on their ears and the music was turned on, immediate physical and emotional connections occurred in their body.

The patient's head would lift from the chair tray, and a smile began to form; for some, the twinkle in their eye resurfaced, and many of the patients started singing, humming, or swaying.

Granted, they still couldn't tell you that you were their child sitting across from them. They could, though, tell you about their best friend in the fifth grade and how they were sweet on a certain person when they were seventeen.

Time after time, instance after instance, the music began to heal. It would replenish the soul and spirit of the seemingly empty shell of a human being. Some people who were under duress would calm down. The documentary was incredible to watch. There is exhaustive research that our music memories are the last memories our mind will lose upon deterioration.

When all else is gone, music is the essence of who we truly are. The research determines, which is where I can barely write about it without tearing up, that it is the mother's heartbeat that is the first music we hear. Sound is the first event we initially wholly experience. It is the mother's heartbeat that embeds in us the ability to allow music to imprint and be so formative in our lives.

I tear up because I think of my pregnancies—swaying with the baby, singing, and listening to Van Halen because that is what made this Mama happy. I am sure my eclectic music choices were why my two children have vast tastes in music.

I could see in her eyes that Becky got it. She understood. Through her experiences of growing up with music and then watching the crippling effects of dementia, she knew that it would work. She said, "I am going to take some Christmas music to my family member and see if it helps."

Music Nerd Lunch

It is a true blessing when you have that one friend, that one person who believes in you before you realize you believe in yourself. The one person who, when you say, "I was think-ing I might want to …" has already finished your sentence. Not because it was their idea, but because they know you that accurately.

My friend Anthony is that person. He and I have spent count-less hours working together, talking, sharing stories, or simply being. With Anthony, there is a comfort in our silence and a genuine companionship in our conversations.

Prior to our lunch, the last time I saw Anthony was during a memorial service for a dear friend of ours. All of us were shaken by her unexpected death. In that sorrow, we reunited and remembered the "good old days."

When I worked with Anthony in Sourcing, he knew how to take the right things seriously. Conversely, he knew when to take situations not so seriously. An example of the latter harkens back to the days when a coworker photoshopped Anthony's face into a calendar to create some of the most hilarious pictures.

I have two favorites. The first was when his face was photoshopped onto a teammate's wedding picture—okay, that still is my all-time favorite. My second favorite was a Jonas Brothers' "Hey Girl"-type picture.

"Alright," I said after I got my food, "tell me about your latest travel adventures." He smiled, delighted that I knew what made him happy.

"Well, I went to see a concert in New York City." He and I love to go and do, seek, discover, and enjoy in our travels. Anthony and I seem to take pleasure in savoring the seemingly small moments: a sunset, a new shirt, or someone's laughter.

Anthony and I have a special musical connection that gives me absolute freedom to be myself. While I know he is not a fan of my heavy metal tastes, I know it isn't because he is judging. Rather, he knows that other musicians will *also* serve my spirit well.

"Heather," he says. "You must listen to this latest Joss Stone song …" Of course, he is always right.

Inasmuch as I love to listen to music, Anthony loves to sing it. He is expressive, enthusiastic, and belts out a song with a passion that few people possess.

As a human jukebox, he can randomly conjure a song that fits the moment, occasion, or even defuses a situation. (Maybe once or twice we disrupted a meeting for this last part ... maybe.)

Anthony and I never needed a club to dance together. Nope. We are *those* zany people who will dance anywhere, anytime, with actual music or something he starts singing. We have danced in parking lots, meeting rooms, office cubicles, and while walking down the street.

Our spontaneity is what drives our friendship. It might also be why we are given plenty of berth in group settings, because others might not want to be associated with knowing us.

When I first told Anthony about wanting to take a Coffee Break, I explained that I would like to try to write a book. We were sitting in his cubicle, and I told him, "The book I would like to write is a fiction piece on women in rock and roll."

Fast forward to our lunch, and he was nearly squirming in his seat at the diner. "Tell me more about this book of yours." I shared with him the storyline, the characters, and the era in which the book would take place.

He patiently listened, pleased to be entrusted with this confidential information. Carefully, he asked me questions to clarify what he understood and even went as far as to offer some gentle advice. "Now that you think Roxie should have this attitude, have you thought about changing it slightly to be more like an aloof musician?"

In that moment, I realized how personal it was to share my creative thoughts, and yet, there was not even the slightest hesitation to entrust him with my dreams.

I blushed as he said in a louder voice to garner interest from other diners, "I will be the first in line for your book signing."

My cheeks still slightly pink, I said, "You know, Anthony, the funny thing is, not only do I know you will be first in line at my book signing, I can also see you carrying the boxes into the venue where I am signing to ensure you are indeed the first in line for your friend's book." Near tears, I choked out, "You believe in me that much."

He looked me in the eyes and, as my spirits soared, he said with sincerity, "You know I want this for you."

At lunch, I am enamored when I hear Anthony speak of his dreams too. He envisions himself singing on a stage with an adoring crowd, the lights shining on his exquisitely tailored outfit.

His passion for singing is not limited to being a solo artist. When I have seen him perform with groups, it is hard to determine what brings him more joy, solo or ensemble artistry. While the spotlight is an enviable position, Anthony finds tremendous joy in being the person who lifts others up, encouraging vocal exploration and finding achievement in a group setting.

There are "somedays" out there in Anthony's and my future where we will willingly travel to see the other achieve their dreams. On those days, I will be lugging his sound equipment to center stage, and conversely, he will be carrying my boxes of books.

Each of those days will be grand.

The Wrap-Up

This desire to visit wild and wonderful places continued into my adulthood. My Coffee Break was the perfect opportunity to scratch the travel itch and journey to some United States cities I hadn't previously visited.

It is the rare person who takes a sabbatical and does not travel. It seems to be a universally expected rule that one must travel when taking a break. I understood the implied requirement and fulfilled my duty.

One of the goals I set for myself during my Coffee Break was to get to Muscle Shoals, Alabama. The music documentary *Muscle Shoals,* set in that area, intrigued me. I wanted to see this mysterious and alluring area on the Tennessee River where music by famous musicians such as the Staple Singers, Aretha Franklin, The Rolling Stones, Paul Simon, and Julian Lennon was recorded, a song or two, and in some unanticipated cases, entire albums.

Many of these albums went on to critical acclaim or popularity. In its heyday, there were twenty active recording studios in Muscle Shoals. Now that number is about ten or twelve.

As I zoomed out on the map in that part of the southeastern United States, I realized how close Nashville was to Muscle Shoals, and how close Memphis was too. Those were both excellent music cities.

Expanding the map further, I realized that if I was going to those cities, I might as well go to New Orleans. And, if I were to go to New Orleans, I should travel to Austin, Texas. My accidental bucket list music trip was created and, more importantly, implemented.

The eleven-day trip was nothing short of incredible. I began the trip as one should for music history purposes: in Memphis, Tennessee, with soul music.

On Fridays in September, the Civil Rights Museum hosted the MLK Soul Concert Series.

From the first note, I knew immediately this was the most appropriate way to begin my music journey. While in Memphis, I also made stops at the Rock 'n' Soul Museum, Stax Music Studios, Sun Records, and, of course, Graceland.

Next was Muscle Shoals. It lived up to the lore from the documentary. I toured three studios. I saw the receipt for the Rolling Stones' "Wild Horses" recording session. I walked past the Wurlitzer, made famous by the Staple Singers. I stood in the studio where Percy Sledge recorded "When a Man Loves a Woman." I stood on the famous rock in the Tennessee River where Julian Lennon was inspired to pen "Valotte."

In Nashville, while I'm not a big country music fan, I still had a great appreciation for the live music that was available almost 24/7. My favorite stop in Nashville was the Johnny Cash Museum.

My visit to New Orleans was one of my biggest music highlights ever with my time at Preservation Hall. Established in the 1960s, the name is precisely the intention: a small music venue dedicated to the preservation of the original brass band sound.

Perhaps 100 people can fit into this tiny, almost invisible space. There was, thankfully, a very strict policy of no cell phones, recording devices, or any such distractions.

When the music began, I experienced sound and music like I never had before. I was wholly and completely *the* music. Every pore and molecule in my body was saturated with it. I sat and focused on BE-ing in the moment.

This felt like a pivotal moment in my life in terms of my music fandom. Usually, music, concerts, and sounds flow through me. However, in Preservation Hall, in that moment, on that day, the music FILLED me.

Finally, my bucket list music trip ended in Austin, Texas. What an amazing live music city. I could not get enough of the small venues featuring singers and songwriters.

As luck would have it, my final night in Austin ended with seeing the ultimate rock and roll show. I stood in the mezzanine standing room only section at Austin City Limits and saw Robert Plant's solo show. It was incredible! It was the perfect way to end my music pilgrimage.

These four individuals all had wild, wonderful, and personal travel stories. Much like my lunch guests, my personal intentions for traveling vary. Perhaps it is for work, sightseeing, or a funeral. Regardless of the why, there is always the what. I have learned that travel cannot be accomplished without some sort of connection.

CHAPTER 5

FEET FIRST ENTRY

"Swimming doesn't build character, it reveals character."

–Unknown

It was the late 1980s when I tried out for the high school swim team. I spent entire summers in my neighbors' pools splashing around and doing more than working on my tan. How much harder could the swim team be? I mean, seriously, for a nonathlete like me. Wouldn't the swim team be more fun than work? I was woefully underprepared.

On the first day of practice, I had barely been wet for five minutes when I quickly discovered that a) I was **not** in shape and b) swimming laps was **very** difficult. My memories of that day are murky at best. Still, I can recall two moments.

First, the fear that struck my heart that I was going to drown at practice, *in front of everyone.* Wouldn't that be the ultimate teenage embarrassment? This led to my second memory, quitting within the first twenty minutes of practice.

Even with my dim memories, when I recall that scene, I see myself gasping, sputtering, and looking and feeling like a drowned mouse. A drowned "rat" would have implied that I had any kind of size at that age. On that day, I was probably barely five feet tall and weighed maybe about 100 pounds.

Up until that point, my last formal swim lesson was at least eight years before that fateful day. And yet, I am still filled with shame for quitting during practice.

Fast forward twelve to fourteen years to the "Baby and Me" swim class at the YMCA with my children. I loved those intimate moments with the kids. We participated in the class when they were only six or eight months old.

Their big eyes grew larger with delight as they smacked the water open-handed. Then, they desperately grabbed a handful of water, only to quickly realize that was not going to happen. Or they would get a silly reaction from me when they splashed me.

Perhaps their favorite moment (and mine too) was dancing around in circles with the other parents and toddlers, dramatically singing, "Motorboat, motorboat … going so slow … Motorboat, motorboat … going so fast! Motorboat, motorboat ran out of gas!" Everyone would giggle and squeal at the ending.

Almost as enjoyable as the class was the extra-long nap my children would take on those days. Everyone benefited.

Our next exposure to swimming as a family was a year or two later in my aunt and uncle's swimming pool. My kids each had zip-up, floating swimsuits. Their arms and legs were completely free, which allowed them to paddle and kick as they pleased.

Both kids looked like fishing bobbers dancing on top of the water. This is where they built their comfort and confidence in the water at two and three years old. They loved the game of jumping off the side of the pool and going underwater, and they were thrilled when the float part of the suit safely brought them back to the surface.

My uncle, when he was selecting where to put the inground pool on his property, was adamant that it had a separate access point. He did not want a direct entry from the back sliding glass door of the house. He and my aunt were determined to avoid any risk of accidental drowning. This made for an enjoyable time swimming in the water for everyone.

A few years after that, when we moved to Seattle, my husband and I enrolled the kids in swimming lessons. My kids learned quickly and moved up through the levels.

Their time learning was great for a couple of years, then a chance encounter with one of Nolan's classmates sent us "feet first" into the world of competitive swimming. Little did we know the friendships we would forge as adults and the lasting friendships our children would have as well.

These lunches provided an opportunity to enjoy each other's company outside of the smells of chlorine, the sounds of loudspeakers announcing swim events, and the scenes of children in colorful swim gear preparing to dive into the blue waters.

First Swim Lunch

There was a scene in *Forrest Gump* when he heard the sweetest voice saying, "You can sit here if you want." My First Swim Lunch was with someone whose voice made a huge difference in my life, and that of my children too.

Lisa's daughter was the reason we even became a swim family. Her youngest child, Haley, and my oldest child, Nolan, had been school friends since kindergarten.

When Nolan was in third grade, he and his younger sister, Bridget, were taking swim lessons at the local pool. One day, Nolan saw Haley getting out of the pool. They exchanged hellos. Then Nolan asked Haley what level of lessons she was in. She proudly said, "I'm not taking lessons, I'm in the swim club!"

Nolan immediately turned to my husband, Mark, and said, "I don't want to play soccer anymore, I want to join the swim club." The rest is history. Since that moment, they have been on the same club team, and even Bridget and Haley swam on the same high school team.

Lisa and I's friendship began when I heard her gentle voice behind me on the bleachers at one of the first swim meets. She tapped my shoulder and said, "Well, you need to get a heat sheet, a highlighter, and a Sharpie. This is how you and the kids keep track of the events, heats, and lanes."

It was obvious to her that I needed help when she saw me flipping through pages, desperately trying to discern what a heat sheet was or how to use it. I was an absolute swim meet novice.

A heat sheet, for the uninitiated, is a paper document that shows the order of events (strokes and distances: i.e., Freestyle, 100 yards), the various heats within those events, and, finally, the lane in which the swimmer was to swim.

This document would then be translated with a Sharpie onto each kid's arm with an E (event), H (heat), and L (lane) for their reference. Each kid would average about three to four events in a swim meet.

Lisa's voice and wisdom still make me grateful for that fateful day. She patiently showed me how to set the kids up for swimming success. Throughout the years, she was my go-to for questions or advice.

The beautiful thing about the swim community, be it parents or swimmers, was that there was a sense of camaraderie and mutual support. We were there for each other when our kids succeeded, struggled, or hit a plateau. As parents, we learned to let the coaches coach our kids, and we would be there with a dry towel, a hug, or both.

Slowly, a side group of parents formed a group called the Margarita Swim Mamas. More about that with a different lunch.

There was a meme that Lisa once sent me, which fits her more than it suits me. "Classy, sassy, and a little bad assy." Lisa has exquisite taste and style. Her home is warm and cozy. She is funny and energetic. And, well, she has a bit of a mischievous side to her, too.

Before our lunch, she scrutinized some dining options. Her research suggested that we try a small bar and restaurant called The Black Duck Cask and Bottle.

It was an adventure as it was a place neither of us had eaten at, yet it looked right up our alley. With the ambiance of a small local bar with red brick casing and large wooden tables and chairs, it did not disappoint!

During our lunch, we caught up on our kids. Her oldest son, Dillon, would return for the Christmas holiday break from college in a few days. She was proud of him for working hard and his dedication to learning.

Dillon did for my kids what she did for me. He helped them navigate the swim world. I enjoyed hearing how he is doing in college because I knew my turn as a college parent was quite literally around the corner.

We talked about college visits and plans for both Nolan and Haley. True to form, she was my mentor for the college application process. She never seemed to mind my flurry of questions. I appreciated her patience with me.

Nolan and Haley have remained friends and teammates over the years. In fact, Nolan took Haley to homecoming in their junior year. That was fun to watch!

Lisa and I love talking about books too. She is an avid reader like I am. Many of the books I enjoyed have come from her recommendations. Her favorite genre is historical fiction. She finds some great options before they become big hits. Or there were quiet, seemingly sleepy books that are anything but!

Through the years, our families have grown close. We've spent time on vacation with them over the Fourth of July. Our husbands liked playing poker or their favorite pastime together (sarcasm)—as swim officials.

Her husband, Terry, and my husband, Mark, really enjoyed working together officiating meets. From what I observed, they were smart, fair, and provided constructive feedback to the swimmers and coaches when needed.

I will always be grateful for that single day when I heard that voice in the stands providing me with direction and help in an unknown world. What has grown from that day is a pure blessing. I am fortunate to have Lisa in my life. Even when all the kids are gone, it's not at all hard to imagine we will still be having dinner, drinks, or laughs together.

Margarita Swim Moms Lunch

If you ever see Trina, me, Brad Pitt, and a 1966 convertible Ford Thunderbird, I suggest you worry. LOL! Trina is the Thelma to my Louise.

Trina and I connected for lunch on a fall day in Seattle. Fall in the Pacific Northwest is a glorious and often underappreciated time. The trees, with their yellows, oranges, reds, and rust colors, dramatically contrast against the blue sky. I don't know how, but I swear the sky is a deeper color of blue in the fall.

Earlier that week, there were moments I would pause to take a picture or simply take in the moment. In the fall, I often recall the children's book *Frederick* by Leo Lionni.

Frederick is a mouse. His friends accuse him of not doing anything during the summer and fall months while they gathered their food storage. He would simply say, "I am gathering my own storage."

The winter months become cold, dark, and dreary (precisely as they do in Seattle). Frederick's friends were tired and weary. They asked Frederick about his storage. He gathered his friends and spoke of the periwinkle skies, the reds in the poppies, the orange in the falling leaves, and the warmth of the bright yellow sun.

When these fall days occur, and even during the summer months, I recall Frederick's wisdom and work to gather my own storage. Those memories resurface when the days are short, cold, wet, or rainy in mid- to late-February.

Trina and I met many moons ago during our children's stints in a year-round swim club. She is one of those people who feels like she has always been a part of my life. This is evident because there is a familiarity when we sit down to eat lunch that needs no awkward "How are you doing?" question. We immediately launch into our conversations.

Perhaps that comes from the fact that she and I have shared endless moments in the bleachers watching, more like waiting, for our kids' respective events. During a swim meet, there is a lot of downtime between a swimmer's events. Hours to wait for fifty-eight seconds of swimming. While it seems challenging, it was a wonderful way to form and solidify friendships for both the swimmers and the spectators.

We also watched out for each other at swim meets. A purely theoretical example might be when Trina's daughter was on the starting blocks, and we were yapping away with each other. Another parent might have chirped up and said, "Hey Trina, isn't that your daughter in Lane 2?" To which Trina turned and then said nonchalantly, "Why yes, thank you for noticing."

After the event, we would collectively sigh, *Phew!* Again, this is a purely hypothetical situation. I swear to my children, this never happened to me. (Wink.)

During our lunch, we caught up on my eleven-day music trip. Trina has been to Nashville and would like to visit Memphis someday. I said, "You must go to Rendezvous for ribs! So delicious!"

It was fun to compare notes about Nashville. We discovered that we listened to music in some of the same venues. She smiled when I mentioned visiting the Johnny Cash Museum, and said, "Did you know that Jeff (her husband) is also a Johnny Cash fan? You two should compare notes someday. You could reminisce on all the things you loved in that museum." Apparently, he and I both immensely enjoyed the Johnny Cash Museum to the nth degree.

With tears of laughter in our eyes, we recalled the day "Heather had had enough" at a swim meet. This memorable event occurred when the club swim team traveled to Yakima, Washington, for a meet. It was an all-day, outdoor meet at a smaller pool in the summertime.

We set up our pop-up tents in a grassy area a fair distance away from the pool. This meet was structured differently. There were swimmers of all ages in the events throughout the day. Usually, a swim meet sections off the day with twelve and under in the mornings and thirteen and up in the afternoons.

Not this meet. Translation: it could be at least three hours between our kids' events. This made for three long and grueling days in the Central Washington summer heat.

There was only so much sitting around a person could do. The meet was held in a one-stoplight town, so there was not a lot to do beyond the pool. The kids were restless, the parents were restless, and the air was warm to almost hot.

I had had it. I declared out loud, "I need a drink of alcohol!" Three other moms, including Trina, had a relieved look on their faces as if I had read their minds.

In unison, they yelled, "We do too; let's go!" It literally took all of two minutes for us to assemble before we were walking the small town's streets on the hunt for a drink. We waited for no one.

A few minutes later, we found a small Mexican restaurant. We each ordered a different variation of margarita and began laughing, having fun, and relaxing our minds.

Even though we took our time at the restaurant, when we returned, we still waited another ten to fifteen minutes until the next kid's event. Occasionally, we relive that moment and get margaritas. And that was how the Margarita Swim Mamas began. This was yet another way we discovered how to strengthen the parental bonds on the swim team.

Our lunch was also a time to remember that throughout our friendship, Trina has seen me at my best and my worst. She is a huge champion by encouraging me when it comes to my running (my best).

She also helped me tremendously in 2016 (my worst year). I became very ill to the point where I could barely take care of myself, let alone my family, for a few months.

Trina drove me to doctor appointments, helped get my kids places, or simply visited with me. At lunch, I told her, "Trina, to this day, I am indebted to you for your kindness and friendship."

In her best Disney-characteresque voice, she said, "Aw, shucks, thank ye, little lady."

Competitive Lunch

Kristine is a dear friend who is another of the Margarita Swim Mamas. She was one of the mamas in that group that fateful day when I abruptly announced at a swim meet that I needed a drink. Granted, we knew each other well before that day, but that moment solidified our friendship.

Kristine and I, along with Lisa and Trina, spent endless hours with our butts glued to chairs, bleachers, or stadium seats watching our children swim. The fun of being a swim parent is that you only need to pay attention for around thirty seconds to two minutes, clap and cheer for your kid, then resume chatting, reading, or whatever you would like to do.

With her busy work schedule, I knew that it wouldn't be easy to organize a lunch with Kristine, so I jumped at the unique chance to have lunch on Christmas Eve. It was a wonderfully quiet moment. The restaurant was surprisingly not hectic and busy, which made me grateful.

Even in all the moments we spent at pools, our lunch was an opportunity for me to continue learning more about Kristine and building our friendship. Aside from swimming, she and I competed against each other in Fantasy Football. Our Fantasy Football league was an all-female group of eight lovely ladies. We had great fun as our focus was wine and football. It doesn't get much better than that.

In our respective matchups that year, I crushed her, and she crushed me. (Wine pun anyone?) We each had very good teams with the occasional off week. "I cannot believe you lucked into your tight ends staying healthy this season! Mine took a rough tumble, and now I'm toast!" I chided her.

She smirked at me, "Gotta stay healthy to win this game!"

"This winter weather makes it seem like it will be a long time until we get to play twilight golf again," I said to her with a sadness in my voice.

She nodded, "I get what you mean." Kristine and I have played a few rounds of golf together. Perhaps not quite as serious as our Fantasy Football teams, still, we find a way to be competitive, have a good time, laugh, and attempt to keep some of our golf balls out of the woods.

We talked about our eldest children going to college. Wistfully, she said to me, "Can you believe they are heading to college next year? Alyssa and I had a great time visiting colleges."

Like me, she spent time visiting campuses and funding college applications.

I said to her, "I know! I think we both can agree that we are grateful for the exemplary teaching staff at the high school. I know there were a few key teachers who helped mentor and guide our kids toward their respective fields of study."

I secretly think that as parents, we were thankful for that voice that echoed our sentiments, yet was embraced by our kids. Yep, we are part of the "smirk club," where a teacher will say the same thing we said. Our kids hear what they say, not what we said. We simply smirk (and say a quiet thank you to that educator in our minds).

Of course, we discussed our Christmas and New Year's plans. I enjoy listening to people share their traditions and celebrations. Some are festive with lots of people. Others are quiet and small. Regardless, there is something about the opportunity to laugh, open presents, have fun, and share some eggnog.

One topic we covered was how I support the military in different ways. She sat up with pride in her voice and said to me, "Did you know that my brother is considering retirement in the next couple of years from the Marines?"

"Oh!" I said. "Retiring from the military can be very daunting. Here are a few ways he can set himself up for success ..."

As a military advocate, I have learned that the most difficult part of military retirement is transitioning to civilian work life. The word "transition" sounds simple and easy. From what I understand, it is anything but. While skills can transfer, it is the terminology and nomenclature of the two worlds that make for difficult professional transitions.

Fortunately, more and more companies, corporations, and businesses were learning how to better understand military skills and qualifications. While the various military branches do offer some out-processing training, from what I've been told, it still requires a lot of unfamiliar and uncharted work on behalf of the retiree.

At Starbucks, we had the Armed Forces Network (AFN). It is not only an internal employee resource group; the AFN also collaborated with other corporations on how to best find and assist transitioning soldiers.

The logic was that the more companies that banded together and created best hiring practices, the more everyone wins. Not everyone got it right; corporations were still learning. However, it was heartening when other large corporations reached out to Starbucks to see what had been done with military hiring initiatives.

Much like Lisa and Trina, when all our kids are gone, I foresee still being very close with Kristine. Be it crushing her in Fantasy Football or on the golf course, I know our friendship will be around for a long time. As long as tequila and wine are still a part of this world, I know she will be my friend too.

I have learned from Kristine how to apply the right level of seriousness to something. We take Fantasy Football and golf seriously, and yet, in the same moment, we don't take ourselves too seriously. She has shown me when to take a situation seriously, and yet have the humility and ability to laugh at myself when someone (*ahem, Ms. Kristine*) crushes my Fantasy Football team 209–139 (face palm).

A Different Kind of Family Lunch

In our daily lives, we are all a part of many different families. Some are biological, some are social, some are related to recreational activities, some are related to work, some are religious; the list goes on and on. Pam is a woman who began as part of my swim family, and now she calls me her sister, though we are not related in any formal way.

I met Pam when her son, James, swam on the same club team as my two kids. As the natural order of swim families goes, the kids all grew up together. Elementary school, middle school, high school, and now for James and soon my son, Nolan, college. James and Nolan are two years apart.

The boys made excellent contributions to the Medley Relays, with James' backstroke and Nolan's butterfly, generally rounded out by teammate Jake's breaststroke and CJ's freestyle. They were a great crew. Pam and I always enjoyed watching and marveling at their athleticism.

Pam is quite the athlete in her own right. A huge soccer player and eventual weightlifter, her stories are endless and wonderful. That is partly why we enjoy each other's company; we have a lot to discuss. Our lunch was no different.

We started our lunch in a less traditional way than my other lunches. Yet, it was extremely meaningful and profoundly wonderful. Pam's dad, "Uncle Mike" as I call him, recently moved into an assisted living facility, never an easy decision or moment in a person's life. The family and the individual are impacted in similar and vastly different ways. The stress is high. Family bonds are tested, as is patience.

Uncle Mike was adjusting to his new surroundings. I asked Pam if it would be okay if we visited with him before our lunch. He is a sweet man and is always happy to see me.

Before we got to his room, Pam gave me a tour of the facility, and we met some other residents. The few women we met were sweet on Uncle Mike. He has a jovial demeanor and a grand laugh. One can't help but be happy around him. In fact, one woman nicknamed him "Christmas" because he is always spreading joy. What an apropos name.

He beamed when I walked into his room. Of course, I was happy to give him a big hug. Pam and I settled into our chairs. Immediately, I noticed the "wall of fame." This was a large area with many family pictures. It was obvious to see that he was loved by many.

There were also some celebrities on the wall too, people he met over the years through his jobs and travels. He filled my head with stories of meeting this celebrity or that.

I sat and listened to his stories. Then, he and Pam began to talk about their family, as well as various everyday father-daughter conversations. It was an honor to witness that moment.

Suddenly, there was a knock at the door, and the party grew! A friend of his, Ernie, and Ernie's son, Ricardo, joined. The laughter and conversations continued. I didn't need to worry that I was imposing; instead, I became a part of the family.

Ernie and Uncle Mike told stories of their heyday. It wasn't hard to understand that they always lived life to the fullest. Mischief, laughter, friendship, loyalty—it was as alive in their spirits then as it is today. I quietly thought, *I want to be like them when I grow up.*

Pam and I departed and went to a lovely Thai restaurant not far from her dad's place. She shared stories of her younger days. She was the Camaro to my Corvette. Deep down, we are both Chevy high-performance girls. I loved hearing the story of how she owned a Camaro. I wish I could say I owned a Corvette. Ah, well.

We had so much catching up to do. She understands a lot about me and my life as a mom. Frequently, she would add to the conversation and say, "Yep. I get it. I am only two years ahead of you for most things." The decisions, the options.

Since Pam is like a big sister to me, James was like a big brother to Nolan. They carpooled together to swim practice, swam, and returned home. The boys, both excellent conversationalists, talked a lot, laughed a lot, and, most importantly, encouraged each other.

I enjoyed hearing her stories of James' college moments, knowing full well I was about to embark into that world too. He was doing well and seemed to have made a great choice for the college he selected.

Of course, there are bumps and uncertainties. Listening to Pam talk about these put my mind at ease in some ways. She doesn't sugarcoat; I appreciate her honesty. I'm not expecting the college years to be rainbows and unicorns. It's good to know my expectations are realistic.

Pam also gave me a glimpse into the life of an empty nester. Again, she doesn't hold back. "Heather, there is a lot of freedom in my new life. And ... there is also a lot of adjustment." Her words gave me an appreciation to easily see myself where she was.

Pam jokes that I am her long-lost sister. She guides me and shares life's ups, downs, and in-betweens. I appreciate that she is willing to offer her wisdom. Sometimes I can do life the easy way if I know what to expect. Birth may not have made the two of us family, but chance did, and that can be equally as sweet.

Leadership Lunch

When I think of someone who truly walks the walk, I think of Bernadette. It was an honor and great fun to catch up with her.

Bernadette and I have moved together in swim team circles for many years. Our swim parent résumés include club swim team, summer swim team, and high school swim team.

Like me, she is also the mom to a son and a daughter. Therefore, yes, if it were a swim meet, we were there together.

Our lunch was a great opportunity to spend time together and, more broadly, get to know each other. She observed, "Heather, we haven't ever done anything with only the two of us."

I thought back and replied, "You know, I would have to agree. Even though you were there with swimming from the beginning, we never took time to connect outside of a swimming pool."

Her comment was correct. Truthfully, that was one of the best parts of my lunches. My Coffee Break and subsequent lunches allowed me to spend one-on-one time with people I normally hadn't in the past. The dedicated time without swim events or other friends interrupting proved invaluable. I got to focus and intently learn about someone I knew in only one area of life.

Over the years, I have witnessed Bernadette and her husband, Stu, generously give their time and resources to support various swim teams. Whether it was timing, making meals for hospitality, selling heat sheets, or door security, the dynamic duo of Bernadette and Stu was there to assist.

They were always reliable, patient, and supportive. One such example would be the sanity-saving binder Bernadette helped create for the High School Boys Swim Team Parent Captains. It was a game changer!

Oftentimes, volunteers are not acknowledged or appreciated. Right now, I want to thank Bernadette for taking the time to organize us in every avenue of the swim team!

During lunch, we talked about our girls, both the youngest children in each of our families. Her daughter is one year older than mine. In a solemn tone, she said, "Can you believe that our girls have one more year together of swimming on the same high school team?" Then, her voice perked up quickly as she mentioned that her daughter had dreams and plans of being a marine biologist.

We also talked about our boys. Her oldest is a couple of years older than my son. She smiled broadly, "Did you know that he transferred to a different college and will be on their swim team?" I had not, I told her. "He will go from being the coach of the club, high school, and summer teams to being coached. Even though it will likely be a bit of an adjustment, I am certain he will do well." A mother always knows.

I'm a book nerd, so naturally I think Bernadette has one of the greatest jobs ever! She's a librarian at our neighborhood library. When I went there to work on my writing, I almost always bumped into her. I felt like I had a cheerleader for my work when she would invariably ask, "How's the writing going, Heather?"

Prior to our lunch, I learned what a sometimes thankless and even difficult job the role of a librarian could be. I saw an article headline written by a woman who quit the world of books and story time because of the difficult conditions. Difficult conditions? At the library?

Curious, I read more. She told stories of homeless transients, drug use, and calling the police for one reason or another. Her list was exhaustive. I was shocked because it never occurred to me.

Across the table from her, I quietly asked, almost ashamed that I didn't know, "Bernadette, is the library really a difficult place to work?"

She calmly nodded and acknowledged, "I have all sorts of training for different situations. Essentially, the libraries are a haven for the public, whether they want to read, bring their kids for story hour, or get on a computer. Or there are people seeking respite from the heat or cold or worse." She continued, "I am trained in CPR, as well as when to call the police or how to be a social worker of sorts."

My jaw dropped: how fascinating and heartbreaking. Reddening with embarrassment, I admitted, "I guess I don't pay much attention when I go to the library. I now have a greater respect for you and your role. The seemingly quiet librarian stereotype is truly much, much more."

She smiled and reassured me, "Not every day is harrowing."

In all that she does, says, and is, Bernadette is one of the most generous spirits I know with her time as a volunteer and a guide for the uninitiated. She also does it with a happy heart and positive attitude. Plus, her giggle is one of the dearest giggles I have ever heard.

The Wrap-Up

When I quit competitive high school swimming all those years ago, I never imagined it would return to my life in the form of a gift. As I pulled myself out of the pool, dripping and defeated, it never occurred to me that someday I would learn the valuable lesson about determination.

In the world of swim parent, I was constantly a witness to the phrase, "I can do hard things." My children impressed me with each meet, event, and heat I watched. They worked hard, the fruits of their labor realized in their personal bests, lane placements, smiles, ribbons, and high-fives from coaches.

I'm not sure I ever shared with Nolan and Bridget how their efforts inspired me to do my best, specifically with running. When my training was difficult, such as when I encountered a sizeable hill or a ten-mile run, I closed my eyes to envision my daughter swimming the 500-yard Freestyle and my son pushing through the water in the 200-yard Butterfly.

They made it look matter-of-fact. They knew how to do what was required. They didn't complain; they understood the level of exertion necessary to get to the touchpads at the end of a race. Their hard work helped me to push myself and keep going. I worked until I reached the finish line.

When I left behind the community of a high school swim team, I never conceived the lasting friendships swimming would one day bestow on me. The lunches in this chapter demonstrated that though I quit swimming when I was a teenager, swimming never quit on me.

Swimming waited all this time. I had to be ready for all the gifts it wanted to shower on me: resolve, determination, and deep-lasting friendships.

CHAPTER 6

LAUGHTER, TEARS, AND SHARED EXPERIENCES

"There are no strangers here; only friends
you haven't yet met."

—William Butler Yeats

"Hi Heather. It's Ann." My friend from the Mom's Group I joined less than nine months before was on the other end of the phone. She and I had become fast friends because our husbands both worked for the same company, we both grew up in Pennsylvania, and our kids were almost the same age.

Technically, her daughter was supposed to be the same age as my son. However, she was born six weeks premature. On the day of the phone call, I felt like we had started to settle nicely into our newfound friendship.

Without much hesitation, she said, "Hey, I wanted to talk with you about something. Do you have a few minutes?" She wisely called during my son's naptime, which was quality time for a phone call.

Hearing an unfamiliar seriousness in her voice, I said, "Sure, what's up?"

She paused for a moment, taking a deep breath. "I had some tests run recently. I found out that I have breast cancer."

To this day, I cannot explain why my first thought was, *Today is April 1; if this is her idea of an April Fool's joke, I will kill her! And our friendship is over! This is not funny.*

Keeping that thought as an inside voice was an uncharacteristically brief moment of wisdom on my part. As she continued, I realized she was very serious. The date had nothing to do with the phone call.

With the blood pounding in my ears, I found it difficult to listen to her. Then a moment of cruelty hit me hard: *Our babies weren't even one-year-olds!*

I sat back on the couch and exhaled quietly. Once I regained my composure, I began paying closer attention to her words … *fixing my bra … felt it and thought—weird … checked in the shower … was certain …*

She explained how she found it, the test to identify and confirm her suspicions, and what was next. *Chemo. Radiation. Then see how I am.*

It's strange how when someone shares something life-changing with you, your brain only remembers the big words, not the details in between. The thoughts in my head spun. *This is impossible! She is in her mid-thirties! This can't be happening!* And yet, it very much was.

Breast cancer did not care that her baby girl was in diapers.

The collective group of women from our Mom's Group sprang into action. We cooked meals, helped with the kids, and spent time with Ann. It was a tremendous realization of how a crisis could meld individuals quickly into a lasting friendship.

The collective efforts surrounding Ann were reminiscent of stories from eras long ago, when women would gather to help one another in everyday moments, such as cooking, child-rearing, or whatever needed to be done to survive.

At the core, this was also a matter of survival. While there was nothing medically that we could do, we could handle everything else for her. That allowed Ann to heal and regain her life, now as a cancer survivor.

Ann is still here today. Her children are grown and on their own. To honor and reminisce, I do my best to reach out to my friend Ann every April 1. I always begin by telling her how grateful I am that she is still here.

No joke.

Lunch with a friend or two is a time-honored tradition. It is an often-intimate moment to discuss worries, accomplishments, and frustrations. Seeing a friend across the table can allow the walls to come tumbling down. Regardless of the time of day, a meal with a friend frequently consists of laughter, tears, and shared experiences.

First Friends Lunch

Jackie and Rosie are my oldest friends in Seattle. I have known them the longest, since the first day our eldest boys started kindergarten. This was about three months after my family and I uprooted from Dayton, Ohio, and moved to Seattle, Washington.

That first day of kindergarten was chaotic at best. The loud, brightly colored paper in the room, the desks the size of model doll furniture, the noise of children crying and parents soothing. There was a scent in the air of crayons ready to be dulled. As I looked around the room, I saw red apples of all sorts, paper, and wood.

I still can see the blue ink on the ragged scrap paper with a phone number that Jackie handed me. Pressing it into my hand, she asked if our sons could hang out after school sometime.

Since that day, both boys have been best friends. Spoiler alert: The boys' kindergarten teacher is featured in an upcoming chapter!

The restaurant was quiet and not very busy. For a fall day, it was chilly, so they had the gas fireplace lit, which added some much-needed warmth.

As the three of us sat down at our table, I said, "Can you believe that our boys are preparing to graduate from high school? Isn't this an exciting time in our lives? Here goes 'Round One!'" They laughed and agreed.

We would get to have "Round Two" when we got to do the graduation stuff all over again in two more years with each of our youngest children. It's not often you meet two friends where all the kids are the same age.

We have experienced a lot together since that fateful day, from highs like the first days of school, to lows of saying goodbye to family pets. Then there is everything in between.

It may be the in between where the friendships are forged. That is the place that warms my heart when I think about all the moments I've been through with both ladies.

Jackie was an early riser, and when I was working my corporate job, so was I. While getting ready for work one morning, I smacked my wet head on the corner of the half wall in my bathroom. There was a lot of blood running down the back of my neck. Ah, head wounds are real gushers, in addition to the immediate pain. My husband was already heading to work. My kids were still asleep. I did not want to traumatize their sleepy eyes by seeing blood.

Try as I might, there was no way to see the top of my head. Who was I going to call to see if I needed stitches? Jackie.

Jackie was the 5:30 a.m. call to check if I needed stitches. She rushed over to my house, already with makeup and hair done (how she did that, I had no idea). She took one look and thankfully did not need to touch my tender scalp. She said, "Yep. You need a few stitches."

She assured me that it wasn't so bad that I couldn't get myself to the hospital after I dropped the kids off at daycare. As quickly as she came into my house, she left. I was grateful that she was awake and able to help.

One summer, I asked Jackie if she could feed my cats while my family and I were on vacation. No sooner had we arrived at our destination than I got this frantic call from Jackie. She was freaking out on the other end of the phone. "Water is everywhere in the lower half of the house. There are like two inches!"

All I could stammer out was "My hot water heater did what?"

Rosie, Jackie, and I have enjoyed quiet moments as my "Hey, let's go drink some wine" buddies. Invariably, our tranquil evening would be interrupted by fits of laughter from our storytelling.

At lunch, we discussed the usual check-in of how their jobs were going. Jackie and Rosie are quite successful in their respective career fields by expanding and growing their books of business. Jackie is in marketing and sales. Rosie is a realtor. In fact, Rosie sold our home to my husband and me.

What I don't think either of them knew was how much I admired them on a professional level. Their happiness in their careers was what I strived to find and achieve. If something wasn't working, they found a way to adjust, change, or improve it. They inspired me to strive for the best for myself, professionally.

They are two giving and selfless women. As a dynamic duo, they volunteered, helped, assisted, planned, and delivered events, funding, and activities for the kids' schools, sports, etc. You name it, they were there to help.

Their philanthropical efforts had a way of attracting equally caring people around them, which widened our circle of friends. The expanded bunch possessed similar characteristics to Jackie and Rosie—warm, caring, funny, vibrant, and passionate.

Rosie, Jackie, and I have a way of finding carpe diem in our lives. Yes, some things are very planned, like a vacation. Yet, these two are very good for a "Hey, I know this is last minute, would you like to ..." Spontaneity tends to be our mantra.

Go Cougs! Lunch

Living in the Pacific Northwest, it is a frequent occurrence when seemingly out of the blue, someone will startle the quiet of a walk or grocery store visit with a shout of "GO COUGS!" which is immediately met with a reply of "GO COUGS!"

The alums from Washington State University (WSU) are a fervent group, often referring to Pullman, Washington, as *home* to this geographically isolated area. This likely lends itself to their unofficial motto, "Cougs help Cougs."

Pullman is in the Palouse region of eastern Washington. The beautiful Palouse, with its rolling hills. The place that must be the inspirational setting for *America the Beautiful* with its amber waves of grain. Whitman County, where Pullman and WSU are located, is the top-producing wheat county in the United States.

The Pullman sunsets are stunning. The fine dust particles from the wheat crops create skies of brilliant pink, orange, and red as the sun sets and the blue of night starts to creep in from high above. The colors stretch like taffy pulled across the skyline.

Krista emulates the credo of a Washington State University Cougar alumnus. She is a die-hard fan, quick to wear her crimson and gray, and she knows how to welcome someone immediately.

When Krista and I met for lunch, there was a brief moment of mild clumsiness. We both stammered out, "Is this really the first time we have ever had lunch with only the two of us?"

We awkwardly shifted in the booth seating at the Thai restaurant with its familiar sounds of woks being scraped, water features adding to the ambient sound, and colorful decorations tastefully scattered around the restaurant.

I said, "How could it be that we have known each other for ten years and have never taken the time to dine alone? I guess we were usually in some sort of group setting?"

Our exhale and laughter broke the strange realization. Knowing that this was the first time we spent one-on-one took on new meaning. We understood that with this lunch, we were given the opportunity to learn more about the other person with no interruptions.

Krista and I were introduced by her best friend, Becky, also a WSU alum and the same Becky who was in my travel chapter.

The last time I saw Krista was at a holiday party. I enjoyed hearing about her holiday traditions and the great time she had visiting with family and friends. As chaotic as the holidays were, I saw her face light up with a bit of gratitude for spending time, no matter how hectic, with those who knew her best.

Krista has the reputation for being a "nice person." (She groans at the title; her husband laughs.) Our lunch solidified her reputation as she listened and responded.

One unique feature about Krista, and likely why she has the reputation as nice, is that she doesn't try to outdo a situation. If she had a similar experience, she would share her knowledge and experience and continue to listen to what the other person was saying.

We talked about our extended families, comparing notes on what it was like to be one of many. When I explained my family, especially how many of us there were (my mom was one of thirteen children, and my dad was one of eight), most people's eyes grew wide. Krista understands, as her husband (also a WSU alum) had a large family too. Being a member of a large family is a distinctive experience in itself. Fun—yes. Unique—absolutely.

We discussed our experiences of getting pregnant and having kids. Krista's kids are a few years younger than mine. Her children are nineteen months apart, and mine are twenty months apart.

While we each knew people with kids closer in age, there was a mini camaraderie in having someone who understood the less than two-year age difference. When you first start, it's tiring. As the siblings grew, they easily had a buddy.

I shared how my Coffee Break was coming along. With disbelief in my voice, I said, "I never expected to be this busy, and yet I am! By far, though, the biggest benefit of my Coffee Break has been the ability to get rest and completely detach from my job."

She sighed wistfully, "I wish my company offered that benefit."

Fully engaged in our conversation, we leaned forward in the booth and talked about how hard it can be to manage a family, a marriage, and physical exercise. It wasn't easy. Yet, finding the time made a world of difference. I'm a huge advocate for anyone who wants to work out, run, bike, and improve their health.

Our lunch allowed us to do something we had never done before: spend time with just the two of us.

I am fortunate to have Krista in my life. When we do go to parties, get-togethers, and celebrations, she is always the person I seek out. We have plenty to talk and laugh about. Now, we have a deeper connection in our friendship, and I am that much better for it.

GO COUGS!

Flexible Lunch

When my neighbor Shannon and I planned our lunch for the week, I don't think either of us expected to have to change it so radically. We had intended to have lunch at a local restaurant. Then came the snow.

Quite rapidly, something like four to six inches fell from the sky and landed in our yards and on the streets. Some people would think, *HA! That's it? Only four to six inches. Why would that change anyone's plans?*

The issue was that the Seattle area of the Pacific NW was not equipped to handle multiple inches of snow. There are precious few snowplows and snow removal vehicles. To further complicate the roads, there was a high likelihood that beneath the fluffy stuff was a decent layer of ice.

For the first time, I had my lunch for the week *at* someone's home. Not that I was opposed to the idea, it simply hadn't been something that I'd considered or, in this case, necessitated. Between my upcoming travel plans and her work schedule, we didn't have the chance to reschedule for another day.

There is a silence that occurs after a hefty snowfall. It was divine to be outside in the calm and quiet. Trudging down our street, bundled up in boots, coat, hat, and gloves, I showed up with pulled pork sandwiches, coleslaw, and Fritos. Have food, will travel.

Shannon was playing the perfect winter day station on Pandora. It was the Orchestral Maneuvers in the Dark (OMD) Station. There were so many good songs playing during our lunch. We each shared how certain songs contained special meanings.

To my delight, I heard some songs I hadn't heard in a long time. When The Cure's "Pictures of You" played, I leaned back in my chair, smiled, inhaled, and was transported back to the day that song became meaningful to me.

Bringing her along into my memory bank, I began, "'Pictures of You' is my 'Happy Place' song. I remember one gorgeous October fall day when I was a freshman in college in northwestern Pennsylvania. The sun was warm and in full display against a cloudless sky. A friend of mine suggested we blow off some steam by going for a drive. Who doesn't need a long drive and good tunes to help recenter?

"As we drove through the sunny countryside, the oranges, reds, and yellows were in full show—bright, vibrant, and almost determined to outdo the leaf next to it, contrasting the brilliant blue sky.

"With the window down, the smell of fall was in the air. At some point, 'Pictures of You' came on the radio. It felt like the quintessential song to capture that precise moment and forever lock it into my brain. To this day, that memory is still stored in all five of my senses."

Quietly, I exhaled, grateful that the memory was still as vivid during our lunch as the day it happened.

Shannon and I talked about her son, who was a brass instrument musician. He is the kind of person who isn't satisfied with knowing how to play only one instrument. If it were a brass instrument, he wanted to learn how to play them all: the trombone, trumpet, tuba, etc.

I am always amazed when I meet people like that. Their thirst to challenge themselves and learn more is incredible. Some people can barely learn one instrument; her son knew how to play at least three or four already.

As if on cue, he stopped in the dining area where we were eating. It was a delight to see and talk briefly with him. He falls right between my two kids in terms of age and grade level.

He was no longer the shy young boy I knew all those years ago when they first moved to our street. He was becoming a "man-child"; his voice was changing, he was growing taller before my eyes, and his hobbies were changing.

We talked about Shannon's job. She was a phlebotomist for the local vampires (I'm kidding!), I mean blood bank. I was envious of her part-time schedule. There were many days when I thought I would like to have part-time hours.

An additional benefit of having lunch at Shannon's house was that I also got to briefly catch up with her husband. He and I are huge rock music fans. It was great fun to talk about music and bands with him. He was working from home that day, as were most people in our neighborhood.

It was quite crazy to look out her beautiful back door and see the trees looking like someone had taken a can of Barbasol shaving cream to them.

We had a lovely time and spent far longer together than I thought we would. We got to talking, and we didn't stop for over two hours!

Shannon and I didn't let the snow deter us from having our lunch. There is always that bit of wisdom that says that the only constant in life is change. It truly comes down to how you handle the curveballs that life throws at you.

You have a choice: let it destroy you or go with the flow and enjoy the ride. What do you do? What will you do? I hope you choose (at least once) to go with the flow.

Laughter Lunch

If you ever have the privilege of meeting my friend Angie, the first characteristic you will note is her laughter. When Angie laughs, she inadvertently makes me immediately join in, even if the joke is on me! The peals of joy that I hear are infectious and put me at ease.

As with many of my lunch friends, I can't tell you the exact moment they entered my life; all I knew was that my life was far richer because of them. Angie was no exception. One day, I realized that *voila!,* there she was.

In addition to her beautiful laugh, Angie has this uncanny ability to listen. I have always felt heard and understood when I am with her. Our conversations don't necessarily have to be deep or poignant.

When we look back on our lives, it will be the seemingly uncomplicated moments, like this one with a friend over a slice of pizza, that will mean the most to us. There was something so reassuring when Angie was around.

Over the years, Angie has seen me in literally some of the worst health moments of my life. She worked for the cardiopulmonary section of the hospital. Without fail, for almost ten of the times that I have been at the hospital for either emergency room visits or extensive testing due to an unknown illness, either my husband or I would run into Angie in the halls, cafeteria, or on the elevator. It almost became a challenge to see if one of us would see her. (Kind of a messed-up game, right?)

Among the noisy chaos and disinfectant smells, she immediately leaned in with a voice of concern and asked why we were at the hospital. There was something comforting in the immediate situation, knowing one of us saw her.

Fast forward to our lunch; fortunately, it was not held in a hospital cafeteria, mind you. We decided to be a bit adventurous and try out a local pizzeria called The Smoking Monkey. Neither of us had ever been there before, and we had heard good reviews.

When we walked into the restaurant, in addition to being hit by the wood-fired pizza smell, it was as if we had walked into an alternate universe. This was a great little place with a sci-fi, Mystery Science Theater 3000-type theme. Old, colorful sci-fi movie posters on the wall showed x-ray guns, squared-off robots, and aliens with eyes at the end of tentacles. Yes, there was even a stuffed animal in the shape of a monkey smoking a cigar!

We both selected the pepperoni pizza. It was incredible! The taste of dough cooked in a wood-fired oven cannot be replicated. The care and effort required were evident in the flavor and crunch.

Throughout the entire lunch, we found ourselves randomly giggling and pointing to all the different pieces of décor on the walls. Somehow, that alternate universe became our silly, teenage years. A couple of the posters were a bit more tawdry, showing women scantily clad in metal bikinis or barely-there skirts.

We enjoyed catching up since it had been a few months (and no, it wasn't in a hospital the last time I saw her). Her daughters are a couple of years older than my kids. It was great to compare notes on what to expect when my kids go to college.

She was very proud of both of her college-aged daughters. One attended college here in Washington, and the other was in Colorado. What I appreciated about our conversation was Angie's candid approach to letting her girls be themselves. In a serious tone, she leveled her eyes at me and said, "Heather, it isn't an easy path to let the girls be who they are. There is a lot of letting go that you must do too."

Angie made letting go sound effortless, almost matter of fact. She put me at ease with a few of the nagging little details about what life is like with a child in college. "They will need you and they won't; let them figure it out on their own," she wisely advised.

She was excited to share stories about enjoying the moments of being an empty nester, traveling, and seeing concerts. I was enamored by her stories of her travels. Her recent trip to Africa intrigued and amazed me. Listening to her talk, I saw the landscape, the warm, dry sun heated my skin, and I heard the animals roar or trumpet in the distance.

Talking with someone my age about music concerts gives me great joy. Oftentimes, we have similar artists in common, seeing a specific band play at an outdoor arena or hearing certain musicians in a favorite venue, such as the Paramount. I once read an article that suggested that a person's quality of life increases when they attend concerts. There are health benefits to seeing live music. Sign Angie and me up for that!

They say laughter is the best medicine. I couldn't agree more. Laughing together with Angie about our adventure into another time and place was a gift.

Angie is someone who hears me, is a source of comfort, and is especially someone who finds joy and humor in a restaurant called The Smoking Monkey.

Resolute to Be Lunch

I have a few friends that I don't get to see nearly as often as I would like. When I do, I try my best to be as present as I possibly can. In these rare interactions, it is as if I am filling my soul. Valerie is precisely such a friend.

I met up with Valerie in a restaurant near her work in downtown Seattle, which gave me an excuse to drive and enjoy the sunshine. She also appreciated a reason to get out of the office. (I do not miss lunch at my desk days.)

When I am with her, I do my best to be fully present. Unfortunately, I had a couple of big distractions as I was parking and walking toward the restaurant. As I rushed in to meet her, I made it a point to say, "Hey, I need to handle two more texts and then I will put my phone away, I promise." There was something rather freeing in that statement.

We had a great time catching up on her work and my potential return to work. The conversation felt apropos, as many of the diners were also on their work lunch break. People were sitting over salads, talking in suits or nicer dress clothes. She peered over her lunch and said to me, "Well, are you ready to go back to corporate life?"

Until that moment, what I hadn't realized in all these years of knowing Valerie was that she puts life into a different perspective for me. She never made it awkward, strange, or bizarre; it was simply a point of view I hadn't considered before.

As the silverware clattered on plates around us, I found myself telling her a few times, "I hadn't considered it that way." Or even, "Yes, you are right when I look at it that way."

The way Valerie presented a solution was never confrontational. Instead, it was logical and reasonable. As I see it, this is how a good friend should deliver alternative points of view.

Our daughters were in school together and had been great friends since kindergarten. When I spend time with Valerie, it is easy for me to see why our daughters are friends too. Birds of a feather, I suppose.

Of course, we talked about our girls, their sports activities, and the dreaded … gasp! They were moments away (literally) from obtaining their driver's licenses!

The girls took driver's education together. During that time, it was fun to trade carpool duties with Valerie. Once or twice, we would scrap the carpool idea, go as a group, and hit the mall afterward.

As I've mentioned, several years ago, I was extremely ill for multiple months. The road to recovery was long and arduous once a diagnosis had been reached. That Halloween, a month or so into my recuperation, Valerie invited me and my kids over for pizza and passing out candy.

To reassure me, she said, "If you don't feel up to staying, eat some dinner and go home; I'll bring the kids by later." The idea of a low-stress night was perfect for me.

That evening, I found myself happily sitting in her kitchen enjoying the pizza; there was no desire for me to leave. I stayed and talked to Valerie as well as a couple of her friends.

Eventually, the crinkly sound of colorful candy wrappers filled the air. The cold fall air would enter the house as we heard excited voices exclaim, "Trick or Treat!" a familiar sound from children of all ages.

I thoroughly enjoyed myself. Her hospitality was always sincere and, dare I say, simple, "come as you are," laid back. I can't help but savor those moments.

The night wore on, and the trick-or-treaters waned. Fatigue began to set in, so the kids and I left. When we got home, both of my kids commented on how proud they were of me for making it through the evening. They weren't being disrespectful; they were being honest. Their worry for my health was abundantly evident. That night, Valerie helped bring me to a turning point, and my kids took notice. It was such a great feeling!

Valerie and I are also connected by the fact that our husbands work for the same company. I cannot even begin to express how wonderful it is to have an ally in her. We make the best of it when the guys start talking shop ... In the words of Skipper the Penguin from *Madagascar,* "Smile and wave, boys, smile and wave."

We both aspire to vacation in Australia someday with our spouses, or if they must work, Valerie and I will go along for the ride. I am certain she would be a great travel companion due to her sense of adventure, self-confidence, and sense of humor. All are essential elements in a fellow traveler.

Valerie and I also share a great passion for excellent wine (and let's admit it, food, too)! She originally hails from California, so she has known the best of both wine worlds in the United States: California and Washington.

We like to share notes about different vineyards and wines. She has introduced me to some new wineries to try. I look forward to a day when we take a wine tasting trip to one of the wine regions in the Pacific Northwest. And, if we must, we shall board a plane and go to Spain to compare wines. Woe is us—a traveling we shall go!

Valerie is the friend in my life who fills my soul and helps me see life from a different perspective. She is genuine and warm. A friend who has that spirit with whom I could travel across the street, the state, the continent, or the world and have the best time. ¡Salud!

The Wrap-Up

When a person is asked what the word *connection* signifies, the chances are very high that they will say "friendship." Some friendships sustain, some wane and fall by the wayside, and others are reignited with a single moment of vulnerability.

Recently, I had a friendship reignited. She was my best friend from elementary school. We were inseparable for four years.

But slowly, the dynamics of our friendship changed. When we went to different high schools, we nearly lost contact with each other, save for some mutual acquaintances. With college, marriage, and parenthood, we completely drifted apart. It seemed like the natural order of things.

Then we had an occasion where we reunited several years ago. The reunion was awkward and forced. We had grown too far in different directions and had no idea how to bridge, let alone repair, that gap.

Years went by, and then, out of the blue one day, I received a message from her. She apologized for the awkward reunion, explaining what she thought happened on that fateful day. She asked for a second chance to connect.

I nearly wept when I read her note. The relationship that I believed was no longer alive still had the tiniest of embers glowing. I carefully breathed air into the moment. Yes! I would love to reconnect.

Few words can adequately describe the moment when our second chance became a reality. The world seemed to stop. It was the two of us again; we were young and old at the same time, giggling girls and knowing mothers.

How did I gain a new friend who was still my friend from my youth? I don't need to question it; I simply need to be grateful and embrace the second opportunity as the blessing it is.

Friendship is the cornerstone of human connection. My lunches with these friends strengthened the foundation, allowed for discoveries, and forged deeper bonds. We have known each other long enough to laugh and cry together, and to be vulnerable, if only for a few bites of a meal.

CHAPTER 7

TEACHERS, COACHES, AND MENTORS

*"Better than a thousand days of diligent study
is one day with a great teacher."*

–Japanese Proverb

When I started first grade, I had a very difficult time adjusting during the first several days of school. I cried every day. I don't know exactly what I cried about; I do recall how I got over the fear.

My teacher, Mrs. G, was in her first year of teaching. She was kind and seemed to have a good hold on the classroom. Well, all except for the one kid who would not stop crying—me.

Perhaps it was the grind of an all-day class. Perhaps it was a school where I didn't know many of the kids because I transferred from public to private school. Possibly it was because I was a very small child, and maybe even those tiny desks still felt giant. I don't remember what the problem was. I only remember I was disruptive.

Everyone wanted to help—my parents, the principal, and other students—but no one knew how to help me.

Likely at her wits' end, Mrs. G had a heart-to-heart talk with me. "Heather," she said, "this is my first year of teaching, so I am new too. Do you know that I am scared like you are?"

I shook my head, no. I'm sure in my five-year-old mind, I never envisioned that adults could fear anything.

"What is your favorite treat to eat?" she continued.

"Popcorn," I replied (and would still reply if asked the same question today).

She said, "I tell you what, let's make a deal. If you don't cry and can be brave, and I don't cry and can be brave, even though we are both new and scared, how about I write a letter to your parents? I will tell them how well we both did and that you should receive your special treat."

Through welling tears in my eyes, in my first-grade brain, I understood that her bargain was a great idea for me. I worked diligently for the rest of that week, trying not to cry. I'm sure she worked hard too.

By Friday, I had successfully not cried at all for two days in a row. True to her word, she showed me the letter she was going to put into my backpack. *I am happy to report that Heather has not cried at all for the past couple of days. I told her I would write you this note so that you could make her favorite special treat ... popcorn.* Her trick worked!

I don't think I ever cried again in school until my first day or two of college. Funnily enough, it was because I was only seventeen when I started college. It was overwhelming to be on a university campus, and I wasn't even a legal adult. For some reason, that mattered to me.

My mom wanted me to at least try to complete my first semester. "If it's too overwhelming or not a good fit, you can come home, and we can figure something else out."

Much like first grade, I was determined to figure it out. Popcorn, even the gross microwave kind (versus air-popped), was a good reward. My resolve saw me through that first semester and the duration of my college years.

Fortunately, the lunches in this chapter were more than popcorn. Each time I sat across the table from one of these individuals, they enamored me with who they were and what they did. This collective group allowed me to appreciate the efforts and rewards involved with teaching, coaching, and mentorship.

Preschool Lunch

My lunch with Amy was a huge step up from when we used to eat lunch together. The old days when we carefully opened our milk cartons, and used yellow divided trays to get cooked carrots and buttered noodles from the likes of our lunch ladies.

It was a long time coming to have this lunch with my friend Amy. She and I have been friends since kindergarten. Considering that was only two years ago … I am kidding! I will not divulge how long ago that really was for us. What matters is that after all these years, we are still friends!

The location of this lunch was as rare as having a friend still in my life since kindergarten. We had lunch at a beautiful little winery about an hour outside of … Las Vegas!

Pahrump Valley Winery discovered that they could grow Zin-fandel, Syrah, and Barbera grapes. As expected, their growing season was short, from March to July. They harvest the red lovelies and crush them immediately. It was a boutique winery with limited production. They brought in white grape options from California to balance out their inventory offerings.

Even though Amy had lived in the Las Vegas area for over twenty years, she hadn't been to this part of the state. The beautiful winter day was about sixty degrees, with sunshine and the standard inclement wind. Dust was constantly scattered across the road as she drove her SUV.

Despite the wind, the drive to the winery was exquisite. I absorbed the beauty of the rugged reds and oranges that made up the hilly, rocky terrain. The contrast of the blue sky against the desolate landscape was a sight to behold.

As Amy drove, we visited memory lane. We talked about our elementary school days, and finished each other's memories when we recalled hanging out with her cousin or certain friends. It struck me as both funny and comforting that we shared some of the same memories.

We enjoyed a delicious lunch, both of us choosing portobello mushroom sandwiches. The setting felt perfect: a quiet table on the enclosed veranda overlooking the vines and a small outdoor stage that hosts intimate concerts.

This was a genuine improvement from the basement lunches we shared during our elementary and middle school years. Not to mention lunches in high school with the jukebox always playing The Doors' "Touch Me." Every. Single. Day. (I still can't stomach The Doors because of that jukebox.)

We also spent time catching up on the latest developments in our lives. Amy's days were spent with ankle-biters of either the four-legged or two-legged kind. She amazes me with all that she does. Her heart is forever giving.

She astounded me with her work as a foster mom for dogs. It is a thankless job and not always easy, yet it can be very rewarding. I don't remember the number of dogs she has fostered, but *copious* seems about right.

She was careful and attentive to ensure the right dog was placed with the right owner. When that perfect match happened, it was a wonderful feeling for her. She has her own great brood of dogs. Each dog, while different, is very sweet and attentive.

And yes, like all pets, hers could be little stinkers now and again, especially with toilet paper strewn through the hall.

Amy is a preschool teacher. Hers is, without a doubt, an under-appreciated career. Amy teaches at an at-risk school, where she encounters a lot of students with a range of disadvantages.

My mouth dropped when she said, "Heather, some of my kid-dos start school without even knowing there is an alphabet or how to spell, let alone write their name."

She paused to let me absorb what she said. Then she continued, "When they leave my care at the end of the year, they are fully prepared to become kindergartners. They know how to spell and write their name, how to tie their shoes, how to say their ABCs, and how to do simple math."

"I love my job also because Teddy gets to come with me one day a week," she added. She invested time to train her dog, Teddy, to be an emotional support therapy animal. On Fridays, she and Teddy go to the school to work with those children who need a friend (especially a furry one) the most.

As the sun gently shone through the delicate white curtains, I recognized that I was most fortunate to have lunch with someone who grasped where I grew up and *how* I grew up.

I often wonder what my Seattle friends think when I say I grew up in coal mining country. I doubt they can appreciate what that meant.

Did they know how remote we were from the city? Did they get that we didn't have to travel far to be on ski slopes? Did they understand that Amy and I knew precisely where Flight 93 went down? Did they know the fun we had dancing at La Ritz? Or how we had to memorize prayers in the fourth grade? Did they know the heartache we endured when our fellow Girl Scout died unexpectedly from a heart condition at age ten? Or that our entire second-grade class had chicken pox for our First Holy Communion? Did they know that I remember when Amy sang for a school play, and I still recall her incredibly beautiful voice? Or the day she selflessly helped me get ready for senior prom, and how I felt stunning because of her abilities? Amy knows all of that.

Our lunch was indeed radically different from our childhood years. However, there is something to growing up and growing old. We often complain about adulting, yet it is a gift. Not everyone gets to age, like our young Girl Scout friend. Not everyone lives in the same hometown until college. And sadly, not everyone remains close to those who knew them in their youth.

Amy's life is dedicated to fostering. Whether it is four-legged animals or four-year-old children, hers is a life of education and nurturing. There is no way we would have ever known our paths when we were kids. It is an honor to see the one she has led, as well as walk with her from time to time.

Kindergarten Lunch

There are some people in my life whom I will forever call by their formal name. Mrs. H is one such person. She was the kindergarten teacher for both of my kids.

After greeting each other with a warm hug, we sat down to lunch, and she said, "Please, call me Elaine; you've known me for far too long now."

I stumbled out a reply, "Okay, Mrs. H, I will call you Elaine."

Elaine was one of the very first people I met when we moved to the Pacific Northwest in June 2006. My son was five and would be entering kindergarten in the fall. My daughter was three. I enrolled him in the all-day kindergarten option, even though it felt quite late in the registration process. As luck would have it, he was accepted into the program.

Grateful for a quiet restaurant, I did my best to recall those first days of kindergarten for both my children. "Elaine, what I remember most was your kindly presence and sense of control in the classroom. You were exceptionally prepared in both instruction and regimen. I knew Nolan would indeed benefit both personally and academically with this type of person in his life."

Even at age five, he did his best with people who were strict yet compassionate and sweet. She had easy and simple rules; in return, she was fair and kind. Mrs. H established the litmus test against which I would judge all future teachers.

When my daughter, Bridget, began kindergarten, she adapted to Elaine's style of teaching with ease. Having already been through a year with Nolan, Bridget's experience was equally positive. She grew and flourished in her studies and learning.

Having lunch with Elaine meant that we would talk about books and reading. Elaine is a voracious reader. In the calm of the restaurant, she proudly declared, "I usually have about three to four books going at the same time!"

Leaning in toward her, I said, "I am always fascinated when I meet people who are reading multiple books at once. I can't seem to do that. My brain does not function that way. I have my one book, and I only read that." My brain explodes at the idea of multiple books. I can't keep storylines separated.

As if she anticipated our book discussion, she took my hands and carefully placed a thank-you gift for lunch in them. It was a perfect gift—a bookmark. As I turned the beautifully made present in my hands, I knew that every day I would be reminded of her kindness and generosity.

After wiping a small tear from my eye, I said, "Elaine, did you know that your passion for art is what endeared Bridget to you?"

Two years after educating my son, Elaine had the opportunity to do it all over again with my youngest child. As soon as Bridget was old enough to hold a crayon, there was not a safe piece of paper in the house, and truth be told, a safe wall from time to time. (Yikes!) Aside from the basic foundations of writing and arithmetic, Elaine nurtured my daughter's passion for creativity.

When I think about those early days of my kids' education with Elaine, it reminds me of a Harry Chapin song called "Flowers Are Red." In the song, the little boy tries to draw a picture of hot pink flowers. The stern teacher chastises him and insists that flowers are *only* red and green. He fights back and insists that he wants to use all the colors in the rainbow.

Slowly, after being told he is wrong over and over, he begins to give up on coloring. Then, one day after the little boy moved to a new town, as fortune would have it, he had a new teacher with a bright smile and a cheery attitude. She instructed the class to use all the colors available because it is how coloring should be done. Elaine is the epitome of that second teacher, encouraging students to explore and find their use of colors in a crayon box or paint palette.

The year between each of my kids' kindergarten years, we purchased a home down the street from Elaine and her husband, Pete. Her landscaping is the perfect example of someone who knows that flowers come in many different colors.

When spring begins to make its arrival each year, I anticipate seeing the brilliant colors burst forth from the earth and the soft floral scents as I walk past her yard.

Smiling, I said, "Tell me how those grandbabies are!" Then I sat back and enjoyed the twinkle in her eyes and joy in her voice as Elaine talked about her family and grandchildren.

She loves being a grandma. Her grandkids were so fortunate; she was the volunteer art docent in their different classrooms. What a cool gig!

No time with Elaine would be complete without comparing notes about New Orleans and Louisiana. She lived outside of Lafayette and still has family there. I could nearly taste the gumbo as she shared stories.

"As you know, Heather, from your visits there, be it blood or by chance, family is integral in the DNA of a Louisianan." Those words were as if she reached across the table and hugged me.

Reflecting on our lunch, it was truly an honor. Elaine was the first person I entrusted with my children's full-time education and formation. They are both bright, articulate children with an unquenchable thirst for knowledge.

I know it is in no small part attributable to Elaine. She was the example against which I judged all future teachers. With the rare exception of one or two, both of my children have had extraordinary educators in their K–12 years.

Regardless of our educational paths, we all have at least one teacher or educator who made a tremendous difference in our lives.

Second Grade Lunch

Nine years before I had lunch with Elaine Two, it was the first day of school. When my daughter walked into her classroom, that moment would forever change Bridget's life.

To clarify, my daughter had two teachers named Elaine in elementary school. To avoid confusion and still tell a good story, I will refer to Bridget's second-grade teacher as Elaine Two.

Elaine Two has a kind smile and a gentle, yet firm, demeanor, even with adults, the exact qualities I would expect in a second-grade educator.

The connection between my daughter and Elaine Two was instantaneous. Their bond was forever solidified when they discovered they both held a passion for swimming. They are still compatriots to this day.

Our lunch was a wonderful opportunity to learn about Elaine Two beyond her swimming past that I knew. Her husband was also a schoolteacher.

As she told me the story of how they met, she radiated that familiar grin that comes with having met "The One," a slight blush coupled with a confident, brilliant smile. "I met him at work. I never imagined I would meet my significant other there! The elementary school systems aren't exactly flush with male educators. John Paul was a physical education teacher."

I knew very well who John Paul was. As luck would have it, when my daughter reached middle school, he was her teacher, too—keeping it in the family!

Together, they have a beautiful daughter who is equally as vibrant as her mama. When my daughter was selected for the homecoming court, Elaine Two stopped to talk to her at the football game.

Bedazzled in her soft pink gown, my daughter chatted with Elaine Two in their familiar way. It was then that Elaine Two's young daughter looked up in awe at Bridget. Tugging on her mama's pants in the cool fall air, she politely asked, "Mama, may I get a picture with the princess?" That photo is still one of the sweetest and cutest I have ever seen.

When Bridget was in Elaine Two's class, she came home one day confused and slightly frightened, as well as fascinated. My daughter explained that Elaine Two's mother-in-law needed two organ transplants. In the best way an eight-year-old could explain, she told me that one person had died, and that was why Elaine Two's mother-in-law could get better.

Ah, yes. A tragic and life-changing organ donation transplant story. I quickly understood my daughter's bewildered comments and looks. I gently further explained the process with an actual example. One of my dear friends and co-workers was a liver transplant recipient. I was able to use Jennifer's real-life story to explain to my daughter what a tremendous gift and, frankly, a modern medical miracle that organ donation is. Once she understood the basics, the conversation became easier.

Putting my silverware down, I carefully said, "I never told you how much I appreciated that you shared your mother-in-law's organ transplant story with your students."

She nodded, "Life happens. Sometimes for the bad. And sometimes that bad can become a second chance."

Of course, I added, "I am proud to report that when Bridget got her driver's license, she made it a point to mark herself as an organ donor." Sometimes, classroom education goes beyond any book.

One of the stories she told about teaching second grade made me laugh out loud in the quiet restaurant. She said, "Did you know that second grade is often the age when students experiment with theft? They are kleptomaniacs!"

I was shocked and embarrassed for reasons she would learn about years later. "What? No way!"

She nodded knowingly. "Yep, every year, I make a phone call to a handful of parents explaining that their child stole something in the classroom. I often hear the gasps and abhorrence in the parents' voices. I gently laugh and explain that it is totally normal behavior. The student is finding a way to test limits and boundaries. They are not doing it maliciously. They swipe pencils, erasers, or perhaps some stationery. All are rather harmless objects. I assure the parents that their child is not a would-be felon in the making." I am sure this is a relief to many.

She says the phone calls would become a bit of a reassurance game for the embarrassed parents because while she does call them, thus the boundary, she is kind in her voice and explains, "This is not out of the norm."

Apologetic parents profusely explain that their kids are not bad or cruel. Elaine Two agrees, "I know. They are testing the limits.

They simply bumped up against this one." Generally, it only takes one phone call to nip the problem in the bud.

Ironically, right before I had lunch with Elaine Two, my daughter *confessed,* "When I was in second grade, I stole this rainbow-colored stationery from Mrs. T." She gushed her confession like I had her in for questioning. Apparently, Bridget was sneaky enough not to get caught and warrant me receiving a phone call.

As Elaine Two was telling me this unprompted story, I debated whether I should rat on my now-teenage daughter. I did not. However, when she was a senior in high school, Bridget made amends by buying stationery and writing an apology letter explaining her theft and guilt. When Bridget presented her with the gift, Elaine Two had a great sense of humor about the whole thing.

When my daughter gets the chance to talk with Elaine Two, she never hesitates. It is always heartwarming to watch the two of them together. They are completely engaged in the conversation. The world around them disappears. They talk, they laugh, they share.

After all these years, Elaine Two still connects with my daughter when they talk. To me, this speaks volumes about her character. Elaine Two makes a difference wherever she goes, whether she means to or not. She truly epitomizes the Christa McAuliffe quote: "I touch the future. I teach."

Coach Lunch

Over the years, many different people have influenced my children's lives. Schoolteachers made up the large majority. While some have been good friends who have supported them, there was a small group that probably made the most impact on their personal development—their swim coaches.

When I talked about my fifty-two lunches, my kids kept encouraging me to have one of their swim coaches as my lunch for the week. Time with Coach Grace was a wonderful moment to sit and relax. Normally, I feel like I prevent her from giving a new send-off set to the little minnows in the pool when I try to talk with her.

Year-round, except for August, Coach Grace instructed the kids transitioning from elementary school to middle school, and the occasional high schooler. Hers was a task in patience that few could understand.

My family and I met Coach Grace when my son, Nolan, transitioned to her group, and then, quickly after that, Bridget did too. For about two years, both of my kids were under her guidance at the same time. Poor Grace. I am joking.

At each practice, Coach Grace would experience the give and take, as well as the challenge and instruction, ultimately seeing the rewards in swimmers' improved swim form or personal best swim times.

She always believed in every child she coached. Would she correct errant form and be strict? Of course. With that age group, I wouldn't expect anything less.

Swimming is rarely a team sport. I am amazed at how coaches handle this. There is the expectation that the individual will do well. If they don't, oftentimes there is no one else to blame. This can become a harsh reality, especially for a parent in the bleachers. Being encouraging yet letting a child find their own path was a fine line to walk.

Coach Grace was a very busy person outside of swim practice and meets. She also had a day job. I was lucky to have the opportunity to schedule lunch with her.

That August day was quite lovely, so the chance to sit outside and enjoy the sun was perfect. Swimming in the Pacific Northwest was often at an indoor pool. Outside for lunch was precisely what suited us best.

Since she no longer coached either of my kids, this was the perfect time to catch up on their recent achievements, especially my son's high school graduation. In some ways, it was hard for her to believe that he was a high school graduate, and his sister was only two years behind him. Time flew by.

During our lunch, I realized that both of my kids were probably very good with numbers, in no small part due to the constant math calculations she made them do. For example, they had to swim 100 yards in one minute and fifteen seconds with a five-second rest in between each of the ten sets. Or some ridiculous mathematical equation like that (ridiculous in my non-math brain).

Conversely, as a runner, calculating my splits as I accumulated miles was always a struggle. I knew where I was supposed to be based on the song playing in my headphones, not the minutes ticking away.

When we got to the subject of my daughter, Bridget and Coach Grace have always had a great connection—Grace with her challenging sets and my daughter rising to meet them. The two of them would constantly talk about what I can only ascertain was *everything under the sun* when my daughter was between events at a swim meet.

Once I said, "If she is being a bother …"

Grace said, "No. On the contrary! She loves asking questions, and I love answering them."

Over our summer salads with vinaigrette dressing, Coach Grace set me up with a "remember when" moment. She proudly said, "I can't remember the exact swim meet (can we ever, really?). Nolan was taking longer in the locker room than normal. Bridget, ever the artist, was drawing with her crayons and markers. She walked up and gave me a drawing of a sunrise or sunset. She signed it and said, 'This is for you.' I still have that picture, Heather."

My jaw nearly hit the table. Wow! She kept a drawing that an eight or nine-year-old made for her. My eyes welled up with tears. Coach Grace's nostalgia touched me.

Naturally, our conversation then turned to the cats we owned. How could it not when she has heard so much about my two little fuzzballs? "Tell me the story of how you got your cats," she said.

I smiled and replied, "My two kitties were feral like their mom. The vet treated them as a rescue because they really were. They were filthy with mites. I wasn't sure they would survive. Not only did Cora and Callie make it through their rough start, but now, as indoor cats, those two know they have the good life!"

She laughed, "We do tend to spoil them, don't we?"

Our family had been very fortunate to have Coach Grace in our lives. She was patient, kind, and fair. She led with integrity and determination. I know that instructing kids changed throughout her coaching career.

Regardless, she made it about learning to be a better swimmer, more disciplined, and more prepared. She celebrated the joy in the achievements and provided care and concern in the disappointments.

With Grace, her consistency made all the difference. Even when my kids "outgrew" her, she still offered bits of advice or observations. She will always be Coach Grace.

Mentor Lunch

When my mentor Tony and I met for lunch, we laughed about how I nearly put my foot in my mouth the first time I met him in person. It was when I made an unfair assumption about him.

This was the part of my Starbucks career when I worked in the beverage sourcing area, sourcing sweeteners, spices, and toppings. An email arrived from a director: "Hi, Heather, I have a field person (someone who works with or in the Starbucks stores daily) who is here on a TLA (time-limited assignment). He is trying to learn more about the sourcing area to help further his career. I'd like to set up some time for you to meet with him. Since he will be in Category (the team that decides the direction of promotional drinks and such), I think he can help with one of your projects."

Rolling my eyes, I groaned. *Lovely. A damned "college-puke" for one of my projects, just what I need.* No, I did not say it out loud; I didn't need to. Apparently, my eyes always spoke for me, too often.

The term "college-puke" came from a boss I had during my college days while I was working on constructing theater sets and general upkeep maintenance at a musical theater building.

During my shifts, this boss often expressed how much he hated working with the summer college kids. In his words, a "college-puke" was "all attitude, with no brains or common sense." Despite his gruff persona, I liked the work of building fake scenery or climbing ladders to set lights for the play that was about to run.

My assumption before meeting Tony was that I was getting a barista with an attitude who wanted to prove something. Yes, I know I am mean and judgmental.

He scheduled the meeting. Within the first two minutes of hearing his vast experience, I admitted to myself that I was wrong.

At the beginning of our first meeting, I learned that Tony was a district manager overseeing a half dozen stores at that time. He was at the corporate location because he wanted to learn the different disciplines within Starbucks, like sourcing, marketing, and even finance.

Cautiously, I presented my idea to make the barista's life easier when it came to the condiment bar upkeep. He liked my idea of using a thick plastic bag with a spout to fill the spice containers at the condiment bar for the customers. Not only did this reduce spice waste, but it also reduced plastic packaging and cardboard shipping. A bonus was that it would save the baristas a lot of aggravation.

From the inception of that project, we became a good team. We ran tests at stores and did additional cost analytics. Sadly, for reasons beyond our control, when other initiatives took priority, we were unable to deliver the project to the stores.

As we worked together, I realized that Tony was a great sounding board. I would ask for leadership or time management book suggestions. Occasionally, he would send me a quote that he found helpful.

After several months at corporate, Tony's career at Starbucks flourished. He was quickly promoted. Even after he left the Seattle headquarters, he remained a trusted mentor of mine. Conversations centered around my role in sourcing and my goals for working in other parts of the company.

He had a great knack for being real, honest, and straightforward. He would sometimes tell me, "Heather, you need to think about it from a different perspective." Or "You can't live with this much stress in your life and expect to be effective." I respected that approach tremendously.

My favorite part about Tony being a mentor was that I knew I wasn't the only person who asked him for guidance and wisdom. He was so highly in demand that he started sending group emails to people with quips or quotes that impacted him.

He later adopted this into his LinkedIn profile. Based on the number of comments and responses, it was clear that I was not the only person to benefit from Tony's mentorship.

He left Starbucks a month before my Coffee Break for a new job opportunity. As he helped some of his mentees understand, he walked the walk, and a new challenge and change were precisely what was needed. Tony became a key leader with a restaurant chain called Kizuki Ramen. We had lunch at one of the restaurant locations.

True to form, he spent the beginning of our lunch explaining in detail the tradition of ramen meals, from different noodle types to a variety of add-ins to include in the broth. I learned a lot from him about what to try and what to avoid because while I love spicy foods, they don't necessarily like me back. (Rolaids, anyone?)

As the black round bowls with our broth, noodles, chicken, and some garnishes were carefully delivered to our table, he was ready to listen to my adventures during my Coffee Break.

He would periodically ask questions that hinted that our mentoring relationship was ongoing. Simple questions like, "What do you think you will do when you return to the working world?" Or "How are you making time to focus on your writing?"

These questions, mixed with my own, made the time fly by quickly. We barely scratched the surface of connecting. It was wonderful to see him happy and achieving a lot in the brief time with this new company.

A few years after our lunch, Tony pivoted to yet another role: Executive Coach. "PERFECT!" I exclaimed when I met him for coffee. He was excited, and like I told him over our mugs of steaming coffee and small, sugary pastries, "I know I am not the only person who knows this is exactly where you should be." He explained that it was a bit daunting, yet he felt ready to begin this new journey.

It was 2024, so our coffee meeting was also an opportunity for me to share with him how I was struggling with my own career path. Almost four years had passed since I worked at Starbucks.

In 2020, I secured gainful employment as a Customer Success Manager for an IT startup company and loved what I did. Then, because of the hits and declines in the IT industry, I was laid off in 2023. I was reeling.

I asked my mentor for his wisdom on how to find a new career. He reminded me of the book *Ikigai* (pronounced ee-key-guy). This book explores the Japanese concept of the intersection of what you love, what you are good at, what the world needs, and what you can be paid for.

"Read it. Then be honest with yourself as you journal your thoughts." His advice worked like a charm; you are reading the results of my personal search.

Whether it is a formal mentor or mentee relationship or something more informal, like what I have with Tony, there is a lot to be gained on both sides of the relationship. I am genuinely happy for Tony's clients. From my experience, I know they are getting a great coach and mentor.

The Wrap-Up

Teachers are notorious for believing in their students' capabilities far before the students realize it for themselves. When I was in third grade, my teacher saw something in me that I never knew existed.

Up until a specific day, I was a wallflower who would have best been described as the quiet eggshell paint in the background.

My teacher was selecting parts for the small class play we were going to do, promoting dental hygiene. She announced to the class, "When it comes to the lead part of Tilly the Tooth, I have selected Heather."

Me? I thought I misheard her. *Why would she pick me? I am the second-smallest kid in the class.* My mind began to race with rational answers as to why she chose me.

The detailed memories of that time are fuzzy and blurred, which is fine because it isn't the precise details that matter. What is important is how her choice made me feel. If someone were to ask me the first time that I experienced confidence and determination, it would be that moment. I was certain she chose me over the other seventeen pupils for a reason.

Practicing my lines with my mom over and over while sitting at the dinner table, I was determined not to let my teacher be disappointed. She was going to be happy that she selected me.

The play most likely went well. As far as I am aware, no Tony Awards were distributed for my performance.

My teacher recognized my eight-year-old potential to do a good job. Her belief in me still feels like my own personal Dorothy and the Wizard of Oz scene, when she went from the dull, gray world, opened the door, and stepped into the colorful land of Oz. At that age, confidence was a bit like that.

The teachers, coaches, and mentors in this chapter instilled a sense of confidence in their students, my children, and even me. They each taught me that I was being a good parent by valuing education, or a good employee by striving toward my professional standards.

After all these years, I have never forgotten my first-grade teacher's kindness, compassion, and vulnerability. To that end, I would be remiss if I did not note that I had a handful of other teachers who helped me see the good in myself, the ability in myself, and the wonder in learning. *Thank you, Mrs. G (first grade), Mrs. M (third grade), Miss H (fifth grade), and Miss G (high school French teacher). I am forever grateful.*

Teachers, coaches, and mentors get a front row seat to our abilities and potential. It was an absolute honor to have the individuals in this chapter share their stories and experiences. I am most appreciative of their hard work and daily dedication.

CHAPTER 8

THE RADIATOR BENCH

"Family faces are magic mirrors. Looking at people who belong to us, we see the past, present, and future."

–Gail Buckley

From the earliest memories of my life until I left for college, every Sunday lunch (unless my family was out of town) was spent at my maternal grandparents. Every week, this was rarely a quaint gathering. My mom is the youngest of thirteen children (my dad is one of eight). Therefore, a lunch with ten to fifteen people at my maternal grandparents' home was the norm.

Despite the large number of siblings, my maternal grandparents' home was quite small, with the kitchen being exceptionally minimal. Barely fitting the sink, stove, refrigerator, and the metal dining table with the white Formica top, that space could quickly become crowded. Often, an additional foldable table was erected in the living room to accommodate everyone.

While the adults sat in chairs in the kitchen, my cousins and I had to shoehorn ourselves onto the six-foot bench at the table. At any one time, there were about five of us jammed elbow to elbow. We *had* to like each other—there was no space to squabble or fight. As I think about it now, it was a huge blessing that we all used our right hands to eat!

This was no ordinary kitchen table bench either. Beneath the painted wood casing where our Toughskins butts were seated was one of the house's radiators. Yes, the source of heat in the kitchen was precariously beneath us.

In my grandparents' latter years, anyone relegated to the bench would literally be red-cheeked and down to T-shirts in the middle of a Pennsylvania January! The heat source was a coal furnace that was frequently stoked to accommodate my grandparents, who often felt cold.

There is a high likelihood that my grandma never knew exactly how many people would be joining for Sunday lunchtime. Though it never seemed to matter, she took to heart the biblical story of the loaves and the fishes. "There's always room for one more" was her motto, whereas my grandfather's blessing over the meal always ended with "Father, Son, Holy Ghost— whoever eats the fastest gets the most!" If you went hungry, it was your own fault.

Of Hungarian descent, my grandmother could wield paprika like an artistic master. Her signature dish and my personal favorite was her chicken and dumplings, with the perfectly cooked chicken pieces floating in the orangish-red broth. The entire house would fill with the smell of chicken broth with hints of paprika.

Then again, there was her stuffed cabbage, which was cooked hamburger meat with rice wrapped in individual cabbage leaves, a true labor of love. Even though cabbage boiling and cooking on a stove top can emit an off-putting aroma, I always knew I was going to eat well when I walked into the house.

Another paprika dish was her paprikash (chicken with egg noodles, homemade, of course). So many flawless choices! I do not recall a time when something was not mouthwatering.

There were memorable occasions when I would enter the kitchen and my eyes and nose would go on high alert. Those were the rare times when she also baked pies. She used real lard and fresh apples or blueberries from her yard.

Flaky, airy, and light, the crusts were baked to the color of a softly roasted marshmallow. Grandma's pies were often cause for all of us to rush through her delicious meals to get to dessert quickly.

It is safe to say that my formative years were spent having weekly lunches. Perhaps deep down, that was what I was trying to reignite. The spirit of conversation, connectedness, and hearty nourishment. Apart from my in-laws, all my lunch guests in this chapter shared time on that bench.

Partner Lunch

From the age of four or so, I told my mom I wanted to marry someone who could cook. Even at that young age, I knew that cooking was not a skill set or hobby for me!

Eventually, I grew into a young adult, complete with dating and all that fun (or not). The summer before my senior year of college, I had a business internship near where I grew up. I was single and not exactly looking for a relationship.

About a month after I started, a couple of women I worked with invited me to Ocean City, Maryland, for a quick weekend trip. We had played pickup outdoor volleyball each week at a local sand court. The idea of going on a trip sounded fun to me and exactly what I needed.

We had so much fun hanging in the sunshine in our bright neon bikinis. Music and voices filled the air. We sat for hours on our blanket, watching people carefully make their way toward the ocean, where we dared not go, as we would have ruined our perfectly applied makeup!

One of the women in our group had a camera. Of course, we took pictures, many with the four of us open-mouthed, laughing at the poor stranger we picked to be the photographer.

We returned to work on Monday. On Tuesday, I got a call from one of the women. The voice on the other end of the phone said, "Hey, Heather. This guy Mark saw our beach pictures, and he wants to meet you."

I closed my eyes and groaned. "Ugh. No thanks. That guy saw all of us in bikinis; he must be a real pig. Pass."

She laughed and said, "Okay. No big deal."

As I hung up the phone, my other friend looked at me strangely. "What was all that about?"

I scoffed. "I don't know. Some guy named Mark wants to meet me because he saw our beach pictures. No thanks. I'm sure he is a jerk. I am not doing very well with dating and do not want to meet anyone right now."

Quizzically, she looked at me. "Mark? Like Mark Cleary? Heather ... um ... he likes to cook." I blanched.

Immediately, I called my other friend back and said, "Hey, can I change my mind?"

I could hear the smile in her voice. "Sure, no problem. I didn't tell him anything."

The next day, we had an off-site company-wide training. During one of our breaks, my friends pointed Mark out to me. I was never very bold with dating, so I figured, *What the hell, why not?*

With an uncharacteristically determined step, I walked straight up to the curly, blond-haired guy in the white dress shirt and blue-and-green checked tie and said, "Hey, I heard you like to cook. Why don't you make me dinner some night?"

"Okay," he said.

My knees turned to jelly. I nearly lost all my bravado. *Oh shit, that worked! Now what do I do?*

A few days later, when I walked into his apartment, I noticed the smell of pasta was in the air. As I sat down on the couch in the living room beneath the scarlet Ohio State University flag and watched him in the kitchen, "American Girl" by Tom Petty was playing on his CD player.

That "Best of" album has made numerous appearances in our life together. As he toiled in the kitchen, he reached up for something out of the cupboard. I thought, *The calves on that man are insane! I have never seen calves so defined and squared off before!* The funny thing is, he still receives compliments on those calves, even from complete strangers!

Mark made me a ravioli dish with a green salad for that first meal. Maybe it was the way we both awkwardly waited to eat, asking if the other said grace over a meal, that hinted that he was *The One*. Within three months, we were engaged, and we married almost two years after that first fateful day.

He has been making delicious home-cooked meals ever since. He is a whiz in the kitchen, which makes me so happy, as cooking stresses me out.

His mantra: "A recipe is a starting place."

Mine: "You HAVE to follow it exactly as it says!" He loves to challenge his cooking knowledge by learning different styles, techniques, and ethnic dishes. I love eating every meal. It's the perfect relationship.

It was important that Mark was on board with my Coffee Break, as I would not be earning a salary. It was a serious consideration, which we knew in our hearts was the right choice. With both of our children nearing college age, it wouldn't be much longer before our family of four would no longer all be living under the same roof.

With his steady support, of course, my husband Mark was my first lunch guest of my fifty-two-week journey. It was a brief chance for us to celebrate my Coffee Break and do something we rarely got to do during the five-day work week, which was to have lunch together. I met up with him near his office at a pho (Vietnamese food) restaurant.

Anytime I have walked into a pho restaurant, the warm and comforting smell of vegetable broth is the first aroma that hits my nose.

This one was no different. My stomach started to growl. The place was busy with customers briefly sitting at the basic metal tables to finish their lunchtime meal and be on their way. The noise of the staff yelling out to-go orders was a constant over the diners' conversations.

Because I didn't yet have a specific agenda or plan for the weekly lunches, our lunch moment was organic. Our conversation during that first lunch was nothing out of the ordinary for us. We talked about some of the people he worked with; I mentioned how I was already getting under the kids' feet. Our teenage kids were quite used to being independent during the day.

What surprised me during our lunch was that I didn't feel rushed, harried, or worried about finishing in time to get back to my desk or a meeting. There was a lot more I was going to learn while I was on my sabbatical.

Mark and I took the duration of my Coffee Break to have several of those weekday lunches. The opportunity to meet up with him during his workday was a treat for me. They were reminiscent of when we used to work together when we first met. I always enjoyed having lunch with him then because sometimes we would talk about work, and sometimes about each other. Regardless, it was a simple way to strengthen our relationship.

Teenagers Lunch

During the early months of my Coffee Break, there were many moments, especially with my children, when I took a deep breath, inhaling the chlorine at a swim meet, and wondered: *How did I do all this before* and *work full-time?*

As the splashing and cheering tried to drown out my thoughts, in my mind I heard an honest answer: *You half-assed everything, Heather.* And I mean *everything*: schedules, relationships, work, etc.

Before my Coffee Break, I became the master of how to work at my job right up until the moment I was needed, like when the kids were competing in their swim events at a meet. The *actual* event, not the start of the swim meet, much less warm-ups.

In the humidity of the swimming venue, shame flooded me with this realization. As my kids swam their laps in butterfly or freestyle events, I eventually made peace with this harsh realization. *I did what I could to exist in a constantly teetering balance between work and home.*

Sitting up taller in the bleachers that were killing my back anyway, that awareness made me appreciate that here I was with the opportunity to BE more present.

There were times during my Coffee Break when I got to drive Nolan and Bridget *to* the swim meets and be there from the beginning of the "Feet First Entry for Warm-Ups" declaration until the final whistle, indicating the conclusion of the 500-yard freestyle event, meaning the meet was over. Because, of course, my kids would swim the hardest events.

As I drove my car to various destinations around Puget Sound, the music we could all agree on was Yacht Rock. *And now a message from our sponsors: That was "Summer Breeze" by Seals and Crofts ...Yacht Rock, soft rock from the '70s and '80s, bringing families together in the car.* I digress.

To get that one-on-one time with my two children was precisely why I took the Coffee Break.

My teenage children are fascinating beings. Without the pressure of a nine-to-five job schedule, I was afforded moments to get to know Nolan and Bridget in a myriad of ways. I witnessed them as individuals, observing how they processed their worlds and, more importantly, the adults they were becoming.

Nolan and Bridget are close in age, being only twenty months apart. Yet they are miles apart in how they process the world. One kid sees it in black and white, while the other views it in shades of gray.

Both are compassionate, and yet one is empathetic by supporting others, and the other holds people accountable for their actions. In their unique ways, they are making the world a better place. They intersect in their creativity and yet are separate in how they express themselves.

Despite seeing the world differently, they both have a sincere inquisitiveness for the universe in which they exist. They ask tons of questions, as is the norm with them. They never seem to have left the "why" stage of early childhood. I have always been quick to indulge it. They are curious beings. They genuinely want to understand. Yes, it can be exhausting always, and I mean *always*, explaining or answering questions. And yet, I wouldn't have it any other way.

They both are academically smart and highly creative. The last part makes me the happiest. When they were first born and began to navigate this earth, my deepest hope was that they would be creative beings with a sense of imagination and wonder.

They have not disappointed me. Nolan took a welding arts class for a few years in high school, and Bridget took a more traditional creative arts class for a few years too.

My kids had never stepped foot on the soil of Slippery Rock University's campus, my college alma mater. Sure, they've heard a lot about it; however, they've never seen it. I strategically planned a trip for us to travel, including college tours of Penn State University, Carnegie Mellon University, and my alma mater.

Slippery Rock University's campus was quiet and empty the day we were there in early August. The cicadas buzzing was the only sound we could hear. The sun was bright with the cloudless blue sky.

As we walked and I showed them different buildings, Nolan piped up, "Hey, Mom, when you went to school here, I bet you didn't ever think you would bring your kids to visit one day!"

Laughing, I assured him, "Nope, that was definitely not a consideration of mine." Perhaps this was the first time they realized that I had a life before their existence.

After our tour, we made our way to lunch. I found it ironic that these two individuals who joined me for *this* lunch, at one point in their lives, literally fit inside my belly. I suppose this was the third way I fed them: first through their umbilical cord, second by nursing them, and finally with table food.

The place I selected was going to be no ordinary lunch, either. Rachel's Roadhouse was an extra-special place to go when I was in college. We had to scrape together and save money as well as plan to go. Now here I was, walking into the brown brick building with my two children more than two decades later. It was delightful.

My favorite appetizer at Rachel's was their soft pretzels. When those homemade pretzels came out with the yellow mustard and cheese sauce, my mouth began to water. Because of Mark's home cooking, our kids are foodies. They enjoyed the appetizer and their respective meals.

In the quiet atmosphere of our lunch, I spent time sharing some more of my memories of Slippery Rock University, why I selected it, what I learned, activities I did, and so on. Seeing the campus removed some of the mystique behind "Mom's school."

As we enjoyed the summer day with the sun shining in through the windows in our corner booth, we laughed, talked, and maybe even teared up a little from some more difficult memories. We shared inside jokes we remembered. We were able to BE.

Our time in Western Pennsylvania was beyond anything I had ever imagined! I truly don't know what I did right in this world to be blessed with two amazing individuals.

Yes, the teenage years are difficult. Some parents fail to realize or appreciate the wonder of the little hints and moments that reveal the personalities and traits of the adults their children are becoming.

Fast forward to today. Do I miss them now that they have left the nest? Without a doubt. Those four days helped strengthen our bond and relationship. I am a proud and happy Mama because they teach me each day to be fascinated, be intrigued, be appreciative, and be human.

Cousins Lunch

The Oregon Coast is a noun, a verb, and an adjective all in the same instance. It is one of the most picturesque places I have ever been, and I repeatedly visit any chance I get. The rugged beauty of a rocky coastline contrasts with gentle green pine trees twisted and jutting out of the sheer cliffs.

Even on the rainiest of days, the Oregon Coast is a gem. As I drove the squirrelly Highway 101, smelling the salty air, a group of large rock outcroppings a small distance from the shoreline added to the breathtaking views.

One of the joys of my Coffee Break was traveling to visit some of my extended family. When I did, I tried my best to have lunch with them. On this trip, my destination as I drove was to spend time in Coos Bay, Oregon, with my cousin Kelly and her family.

If Coos Bay sounds familiar, it is because the small town located on the Oregon Coast was the home of Steve Prefontaine. He was the famous 1972 Olympic track and running athlete. He died tragically in 1975 at age twenty-four. His legacy was marked by numerous running records and tremendous accomplishments at a young age, especially at the University of Oregon. To honor him, the town of Coos Bay painted three murals on the side of a building that celebrated his life and legacy.

On the left side was a black and white depiction of Steve in his high school running tank top. In the center, he was clad in his University of Oregon yellow tank and green shorts uniform with his quote: "To Give Anything Less Than Your Best Is to Sacrifice the Gift." His long legs nearly come out of the painting as he runs on an outdoor track.

Finally, on the right side, Steve was pictured in the heat of a race wearing his Team USA white tank and his racing bib number 1005 tucked above his blue running shorts. There was a determination in his eyes and an intensity in the muscles of his arms. I could almost smell his sweat when I looked at that last mural.

Many decades removed from our time squished on the radiator bench with some of our other cousins, Kelly is one of my two "little sisters." Growing up, I was like a big sister to some of my cousins.

I was a part of their lives from day one. I remember the day that each of them was born. Even though they are about nine years my junior, we did a lot together: holidays, vacations, birthdays, babysitting, and random moments of being together.

Later, Kelly and Alena (my other "little sister") were in my wedding. They still have never forgiven me for the photos with their very '90s hairstyles—big hair with obnoxious curls ... ah, the '90s.

Kelly and I planned our lunch with her husband and their two girls. Her husband, Thomas, was able to break away from work to meet with us. We went to a restaurant in the small town of

Coquille, which barely has 4,300 residents (according to the population sign).

We sat down at our wooden table and chairs when the restaurant was not very busy. I like the quiet that overtakes a dining establishment after the rush of a lunch or dinner crowd. There is sometimes a palpable relief in the atmosphere. Having the place to ourselves practically made for a good opportunity to observe the family dynamics of how Kelly and Thomas juggle work, children, marriage, and their friendship.

"Daddy, I did great at swim lessons today! I showed Heather how I can jump off the side," their oldest daughter proudly shared. At four years old, she is a sweetie who loves to sit and draw with me at the lunch table.

"Way to go!" Thomas said, putting up a hand for a high-five. Giggling, his daughter returned the high-five.

Thomas started, "Did Kel ever tell you about the time when I was a bartender and I ..." Those are always some hilarious stories. He grinned and she laughed along with the stories, knowing them by heart and still finding them funny many years later.

Their youngest daughter squeaked and squawked in her pumpkin seat. At barely six months old, she doesn't contribute much to the conversation, and yet she knows how to get everyone's attention with a giggle or silly noise.

Her children seemed so young. They reminded me of days gone by with my two, seemingly forever ago. I remember (barely) when my kids were infants and when they were four.

I turned to her in my seat, "Can you believe that now my two are looking to leave the nest?"

Closing her eyes tightly, she replied, "Yes, as Nolan's godmother, I am quite aware of what that means: The years have flown."

Spending time at lunch with Kelly and Thomas' little ones made me cherish the moments that were now fleeting with my children at warp speed. Each day, I was reminded of why my Coffee Break was truly a gift.

After lunch, Kelly, the girls, and I headed to the scenic oceanside town of Bandon. This place is precisely why I love the Oregon Coast. The quaint village has unique shops and stores. We stopped at the plastics museum, a place that has turned beach trash into intricate works of art. Bandon is also home to Bandon Dunes, a destination golf course known for its breathtaking views along the Pacific Ocean.

Finally, we stopped at Cape Arago and listened to the seals and sea lions barking far below the bluff on which we stood. If I stood in the wrong spot, I could also smell them.

Looking out over the Pacific Ocean, Kelly and I discussed the healing and strength that can be gathered from the coast. The juxtaposition of rugged rocks and calm shoreline calls to my soul and hers too. The sunshine on the blue water contributes to the magic and mystique of the Oregon Coast.

We also discussed our dreams of sharing a commercial building in Bandon where she would run a coffee shop beneath my bookstore. Perhaps one day our dreams will become a reality.

It was tough to leave Kelly, Thomas, and the girls. I live over seven hours away, which makes it difficult to visit them frequently. It's even harder to leave when a sweet little four-year-old in her softest and most sincere voice says, "Heather, please don't go." She knew the right tone to hit me in the heart.

Parental Lunch

Generally, my trips to Pennsylvania to visit family are always busy, and I almost never get the chance to be a sightseer. Plus, when I'm there, I rarely get the opportunity to have dedicated time with the two people who have known me the longest and brought me into this world, my parents, Jerry and Susie. We also took the opportunity to have lunch and visit two very different tourist locations, one heartening, one disheartening.

Our lunch was at a restaurant called Coal Miner's Diner. This old, large homestead was decorated with early coal mining era memorabilia from gear, lanterns, and lunch buckets to awards and news clippings.

I said, "It is still kind of wild to think that I am a coal miner's daughter and granddaughter."

My dad was quick to reply, "Yes, thankfully, my stint was brief, only about three to four years."

Then my mom said, "Now, my dad's time in the mines was long. His time below the earth was forty-three years. I don't know how he did it. Terrible working conditions, hard labor, low pay, and yet, he did it. He had mouths to feed."

As we started to eat our meal, I noticed a tree near our dark wood table that honored local veterans. Different small picture frames with headshots of people dressed in military garments adorned the tree.

My dad is always quick to remind me, "Heather, can you believe that all the way back to my great grandpa, we have service-members in our family? That is a lot of different people from various war eras. Did you know that in about five years, your grandma, my mom, will have three grandsons all retired from the Air Force?" He beamed at that last remark.

"Wow," I said, "that is an incredible statistic and an honorable one at that!" I am from a long line of veterans.

My mom was excited and happy that I was able to take the Coffee Break. True to form, she asked lots of questions during our lunch. "What are you reading right now (her favorite question). Have you heard about this latest book that I read?"

She always jumps at the chance to talk books with me. She is fortunate in that she belongs to her local library's book club and is a library board member. She instilled in me a value for the importance of the library when I was a child. Neither of us ever grew out of that stage. Like my mom, I generally pounce on someone when I know they are a reader. I love to hear what others are reading.

Staying on the coal miner theme, after lunch, we drove a few minutes to the Quecreek Mine Rescue Memorial. The "9 for 9" was the site where nine coal miners were trapped in an underground mine for seventy-seven hours in July 2002.

Flood waters isolated the miners in an inescapable section of the mine. It took a vast team to concoct a plan to rescue them. My claustrophobia kicked in, and I had shivers when I saw the size of the extraction chamber. Fortunately, there were a lot of farmlands in the vicinity, which helped when the teams devised a plan to bring each miner up one by one. The trickiest part was to know how and where to drill a passageway. All nine miners were brought above the earth, safe and alive.

The bronze statue on the property was beautifully made. A coal miner is depicted sitting and reading the bible held in his veiny hands. His safety helmet has a lantern strapped to it, and a pickaxe is leaning beside him. The statue reminded me of my grandfather and the stereotypical physique of a coal miner, with faces and bodies as chiseled, lined, and hard as the coal they extracted from the earth.

About fifteen minutes from the site where nine men's lives were saved was the field where forty airline passengers lost their lives on September 11, 2001—the Flight 93 National Memorial.

It has taken many years to construct a proper memorial to honor that very dark day on American soil. I wasn't sure what to expect. How do you adequately honor something so intense and a part of the 24-hour news media generation?

There was a visitor center with multimedia displays. Walking and reading the details and information was more difficult than I expected. Don't get me wrong. It is a respectfully created memorial site. But personally, it was distressing.

The worst moment for me was when I saw another visitor, a young mother, pushing a nearly three-month-old child in a stroller. The baby was the same age that Nolan, my oldest, was when the planes crashed into our seemingly quiet lives.

I had to walk away from the news recaps; I couldn't watch any more.

After all these years, I still recall where I was, what I was doing, and the deafening silence that followed. I was changing Nolan's diaper in the morning. I always had the radio on.

That morning, the DJ came on the airwaves and said, "This makes Oklahoma City look like a joke." I scooped up Nolan and ran to the TV, where I witnessed the carnage. We lived near an airport. Almost immediately, the stillness was louder than any noise I had ever heard. Planes were grounded for days.

On September 11, 2001, I held my son tightly, his big, blue, trusting eyes looking at me. I couldn't protect him from the ugliness of the world. I am sure I felt like a failure that day. *What kind of world had I brought my child into?*

On that cold November day at the Flight 93 National Memorial, I was reminded that no matter how horrendous or tragic an event, the universal fact is that life and time continue.

Babies are born, family members die, you break an ankle, you trip on a stick in the woods, you drive your car to the gas station, you eat a delicious meal, you get ready for your oldest child's high school graduation. As my parents and I walked around the memorial, I did my best to remember all the positives in my life since that day.

Lunch with my parents was to experience life: the fun of eating a meal with family, the highs of rescued miners, and the lows of a national tragedy. Time and memories galvanize us.

In-Law Lunch

When I had the chance to have lunch with my in-laws, Peach and Joe, it was a typical Pacific NW February winter day with plenty of dreary skies and rain. Naturally, we were hankering for a perfect bowl of clam chowder. Unfortunately, we had to slightly adjust our plans to a different restaurant, still on the Lake Washington waterfront, since Ivar's Seafood Bar was under construction.

Peach and Joe were visiting from out of town to attend some of the last high school events for Nolan's senior year. They had the opportunity to attend his last High School Leagues and District Swim Meets. Living as far away as they do, they rarely got the opportunity to see their grandkids swim competitively.

Nolan was one of two senior captains for his high school swim team. As a captain's family, my house hosted the Districts' meet carb-load pasta feed.

Unluckily for me, especially since I am not the first chef in the house, Mark was traveling. In fact, if anything, I have been informed by the remainder of my immediate family that I am the fourth chef in the house.

The role of fourth chef came with certain challenges, especially when it involved feeding fourteen hungry high school swimmers and six adults. How does one appropriately plan for the right amount of food for calorie-intensive, growing, and developing young men?

I was deeply grateful to Peach and Joe for helping to cook the wonderful pasta recipes. They knew how to get it all done in a seemingly (although I know it wasn't) effortless way.

The boys sat at the tables, laughing, talking, and devouring the pasta options, frequently returning to the kitchen for seconds and thirds. The smell of garlic bread competed with the spaghetti and sauce. The meal was a success because the swim meet results did not disappoint!

The different events and heats were filled with excitement, angst, and the general highs and lows associated with swim meets. Peach and Joe were loud with the rest of the spectators and cheered as if they had seen every meet that year. When he looked up from the pool deck into the stands, the smile on his face said that Nolan was very happy to have them attend.

Peach and Joe were also here in time to celebrate Bridget's 16th (gasp!) birthday. We had a lovely celebration with her favorite homemade mac and cheese and a delicious birthday cake that Peach made. My daughter was very happy to have them here.

At the new lunch location, Peach, Joe, and I spent the time catching up on the recent news with their family and friends. Education runs deep in their families. Joe was a retired schoolteacher, and Peach was periodically a substitute teacher.

Peach's side of the family had a lot of educators. The vast amount of educational knowledge helped when I had questions or concerns about my own kids' education. Everyone knew and understood the importance of learning.

We often discuss what they are currently reading or what they have read for their book clubs. When I start talking about books, I can't seem to stop. They know this and indulge my passion with a subscription to *Bookmarks* magazine each year.

At lunch, Joe said, "I'm reading Tina Turner's biography."

Excited to hear more, I said, "That sounds great! I bet it is good, like there is any doubt." Peach always makes sure I get at least one or two books from her for Christmas.

My other passion, which they happily support, is my love for jigsaw puzzles. Each year for Christmas and New Year's break, I assemble one or two puzzles. It's an obsession since, at times, I'm usually the only one putting them together.

Recently, a Ravensburger birdhouse-themed puzzle she bought me for Christmas was more complicated than anticipated. Nearly exasperated, I said, "The puzzle you got me this year was maddening for sure! I completed it, though it was an intense dash to the finish instead of an enjoyable ending."

Peach agreed, "Some puzzles are that way no matter how innocent they appear."

Peach and Joe have taken a second act in their retirement years. They tirelessly (okay, sometimes it is very tiring) work with a prison ministry through their church. They both actively volunteer in different roles to help those who have made some unfortunate decisions. Whether it is baking cookies to share, creating exquisite watercolor cards, washing dishes, or talking about forgiveness, they seem to do it all.

Their stories are incredible. At lunch, I told them, "When I was in high school, one of my English teachers volunteered in the local prison's library. This astounded and fascinated me. My teacher then, much like you are doing, chose to relate to the human side of prison. Sometimes, all a person needed was another chance or to know that God does indeed love them." They both nodded knowingly.

Several years ago, they started to make what has now become an annual pilgrimage to Maine each fall. Listening to them at lunch, the stories of their trips filled my mind with wonder and, of course, fall foliage. I could see the yellows, reds, and oranges. I could hear the crunch of the leaves, and I even felt the chill of the air.

No lunch or, for that fact, visit with Peach and Joe would be complete without talking sports! Both are avid baseball fans—primarily as fans of the Cincinnati Reds and sneaking in some rooting for the Detroit Tigers. When they come to visit in the summer, we try to attend a Seattle Mariners game.

This visit was almost all college football talk since it wasn't that long after the playoffs. We had to talk Ohio State football. The family room in our house is adorned almost completely in scarlet and gray Ohio State University memorabilia, including bobbleheads, posters, books, and even Coca-Cola bottles, thanks in no small part (and I mean it is a lot!) to Peach and Joe. They enjoy finding something to add to "The Room," as it has been named.

They feed my passions and, most importantly, adore my children, their grandchildren. I have been very fortunate to have them in my life. I admire who they are and who they continue to strive to be. They make the world a much better place in many ways.

Brotherly Lunch

The lunch with my little brother, Brian, and his wife, Cindy, was not easy to coordinate. My brother and I have lived on opposite ends of the United States since he joined the Air Force over twenty years ago.

Uncle Sam moved my brother and his family around to different bases throughout the United States while I lived in the Pacific Northwest. Obviously, I kept their address in pencil for many years.

After he retired from the Air Force with twenty-three years of service, Brian, Cindy, and their two children established their "forever home" in Pennsylvania. Settling down finally meant the freedom to recycle cardboard boxes and not store them for the next move.

In the over twelve years I worked at Starbucks, I was a very active and avid military supporter. Through the Starbucks Armed Forces Network, some former military members explained the difficulties of transitioning from military to civilian life. They shared that while the skills are the same, the terminology is different. This gap in understanding can make it difficult for a civilian company to hire qualified candidates.

Like a good big sister, I had a suspicion that when it came time for his retirement, my brother would be no different from the people I worked with at Starbucks.

The year before, I took the time to explain how to seek out Veteran hiring programs with different companies. He was able to find a job that moved his family to Pennsylvania.

We were able to get together for lunch because my family, his family, and our parents were able to meet up in the Tennessee Smoky Mountains for spring break in April 2019. It was a wonderful time filled with family milestones and events.

While we were there, April 10th was National Siblings Day. Ah, my sibling. The only individual who uniquely makes the world wild, wonderful, colorful, and above all, he keeps the secrets we don't want our parents to know!

Naturally, my brother and I had some good chiding about the holiday. *Eww. I not only celebrate the day because of you, but I also have to be in the same place as you?* The foundation of my brother's and my relationship is built securely on sarcasm.

For our lunch, we found a fun little bar and restaurant called the Roaming Gnome. It seemed like an appropriate title for Brian and Cindy. Even though we were on vacation, this lunch afforded us precisely the uninterrupted time where we could fully focus on each other. This sports bar had the requisite Golden Tee video game in the corner beside the jukebox, which was next to the electronic dartboards. The smell of fried food hit us as we walked in the door with the jukebox playing a Journey song.

From the first time I met Cindy early in their relationship, I knew she was going to be my sister-in-law. The way she laughed at his corny jokes began to hint at how much she loved my brother. They liked to sightsee and go places together. Sometimes when a big sister knows, she knows.

When she agreed to marry him, Cindy knew full well that not only was she going to be my brother's wife, but she would also be a military spouse. And yet, she still signed up. Through it all, she understood what was required, like moving a lot, and made the best of the situation.

While we ate lunch, the three of us talked about working and good bosses. "My version of a great boss," I said, "Is the one who supports and finds opportunities for me to grow."

Cindy was quick to add, "However, the worst kind of boss is the micro-manager."

My brother and I groaned, "Yuck! Yes!" We then each shared our horror stories of working for the dreaded micro-managers.

Taking my big sister role seriously, I shared, "The important part of a job is doing something that makes you happy and you have a sense of pride with the work done."

Cindy's days were filled with two bosses of a different sort. Among the schoolbooks and lesson plans, she homeschooled my nephew and niece. She was excited to tell me, "Near our home, I have access to an education co-op to share the teaching load."

I said, "Oh! My friend who homeschooled in Texas worked with a co-op too! She said it made all the difference in helping her girls get a more expansive education."

My brother and I are both avid runners. While my brother is the more adventurous one, running 50K races and marathons, I have stayed comfortably and happily in my half-marathon lane.

Brian and I did get the chance to run together while we were on our vacation. During lunch, I said, "I have the North Olympic Discovery Half Marathon coming up in June! I can't wait. It is my favorite race." Oh, how easily runners fall into talking shop as everyone around grimaces.

They purchased acreage in Central Pennsylvania. It was a little shocking to hear them both say, "We want to build a cabin on the property for after the kids leave. We would like to have other adventures too." I thought to myself, *Could we really be this age?*

Funny how our lives have changed from the days as kids playing in the creek behind our house or hiking the trails we made behind our property. Trails so burned into our minds, we can walk them now in the dark.

We have done some stupid shit in our lifetimes. Goodness knows my brother has the stories to explain how he survived growing up with me, like when I told him to jump to reach the monkey bars when he was too short, only to slip and land on both wrists. Or when I was mad and threw my hairbrush at him, knocking half a front tooth out. Panicked, I yelled, "Don't tell Mom!" I still remember the look he gave me like, "Um, Heather, what the hell? She is going to notice!"

Even though I am the oldest, smartest, and best-looking (according to our grandma's preacher), I am fortunate to have my brother Brian in my life. We don't often get the chance to see each other, let alone have dedicated time, like a lunch, to focus on each other. I was very appreciative. Plus, Brian picked up the whole check! Double bonus!

The Wrap-Up

Mark and I have built a life of traditions that have centered around food, meals, and gathering. I would not suppose that we are different from other families.

For birthdays, Mark asks what each of us would like for our celebratory meal. Nolan almost always selects smoked ribs, Mark's "world-famous baked beans," and baked apples.

Bridget's choice is usually homemade macaroni and cheese with baked apples, and mine is any kind of seafood dish. I love living in the Pacific Northwest; it makes my selection super easy! For his birthday, Mark picks any one of those options. Yes, he cooks his own birthday dinner; he does want it to be edible!

When our extended families come to visit, Mark is often in the kitchen whipping up his famous, though not quite "world famous," jambalaya or everyone's personal favorite homemade pizza. Yes, it is sourdough pizza from "Fred," the starter he began in March 2020. Prior to that, it was still a homemade crust that even I could make.

New Year's is my favorite holiday. I love the potential to begin anew, to create resolutions, seek ways to improve myself in the year ahead, and all the traditions!

My family and my cousin Kelly's family have indulged me on my favorite holiday. This means that we have picked up or created several traditions for New Year's Eve and New Year's Day, mostly surrounding food; however, some are fun activities.

For activities on New Year's Eve, the guys put together a 3D puzzle while the ladies work on a traditional jigsaw puzzle, then we play an "Escape the Room" board game.

Finally, we toast the new year wearing red for good luck, with confetti poppers, noise makers, and sometimes personalized etched champagne glasses. On New Year's Day, IF (that is a big IF) Mother Nature is kind, some of us will jump into the Pacific Ocean for a Polar Bear Plunge to start the new year off right.

However, Mother Nature can be sneaky—literally—which means that sometimes we abort our plans because of the dreaded sneaker waves. Those are nothing to mess with; people have been swept out to sea and drowned by them. That would really put a crimp on the New Year celebration.

For food, Mark and Thomas usually cook up a large spread on New Year's Eve. This past year, as the ten of us sat around the table, we all said what we were happy we got to do in the previous year and what we wanted to accomplish the next year.

New Year's Day is a big feast! The table is adorned with black-eyed peas and greens to signify money in the new year. None of us knows the story behind why baked apples are good luck for the new year, but we picked up the tradition, and I don't like knocking out a tradition. I'm that superstitious.

Finally, there is pork and sauerkraut. My maternal grandfather taught me that it is good luck to eat pork on New Year's Day. He said, "You don't eat chicken, because a chicken scratches backwards. A pig roots forward. So, we eat pork because we want to move forward in the New Year." With a side of home-made mashed potatoes, that meal sets the body and soul into the right mood for the year. (Or so I believe.)

My family in this chapter has sat across many tables from me, either in a restaurant or more frequently in my home. It is a blessing and a gift each time.

PART II:

TIME

The Precious Resource

CHAPTER 9

YOU DON'T NEED TO BE SUPERWOMAN

"There is no such thing as superwoman, you can't have everything if you do everything."

−Gloria Steinem

My kids were two grades apart for their K-12 education. When it came to volunteering at the school or being the classroom parent, I was reliably unreliable. Working outside of my home in a corporate job required a forty-five- to sixty-minute commute one way. Despite my good intentions, I never did get the hang of "doing it all."

When both kids were in elementary school, I remember arriving at the school to pick them up for a dentist appointment. I pulled into the guest parking area and saw a metal license plate holder on a minivan: *Fairwood Elementary Volunteer Parent of the Year.*

Sitting in my minivan, I squeezed my eyes shut and exhaled, "Well, that will *never* be me. I will be lucky to get 'Mom of the Year' in my own home." Somehow, I always knew I was short-changing everyone and everything.

Nothing was more evident than the day I was driving my kids to daycare before I caught the train to work in Seattle. My husband prepared the weekly meals on Sundays for us to eat throughout the week.

He happened to be traveling for work that week when a voice from the back of the minivan piped up as I drove. "In our house, the mom doesn't cook, the dad does. That is why we had to *survive* on leftovers this week."

My jaw dropped. "Gee, thanks, Nolan," I said with a cringe in my voice.

His voice brightened as he continued, "Except for last night when you made dinner."

I retorted, "Nolan, all I made was spaghetti."

Looking in the rearview mirror, I could see his sly smile. "Yeah! You boiled the noodles!" Desperately wanting to close my eyes, I realized that boiling noodles was the bar that my kids set for me.

It didn't matter that I was driving them to daycare or that I had all their paperwork for the week in order. Or that I had everything prepared for them to go to their swim meet for the weekend. There was so little that my kids or any kids under-stood about what a parent does to make their world turn.

Somehow, I have to make peace with the fact that I was not going to be like the mothers of my children's friends. I was not going to volunteer for every fundraiser, or any fundraisers for that matter. I was not going to be a weekly classroom parent volunteer.

Motherhood is a tricky and slippery slope. In recent years, it has become even more so. Expectations of academic and social natures run increasingly high, almost to the point of impossibility.

A person cannot be everything to everyone. I could not be *that* mother who did it all: work, home, self, marriage. I became hard on myself, like many of us do.

Inevitably, there comes a time in a mother's life when some gentle spirit throws her a lifeline or, more accurately, a mirror. This kind spirit demonstrates and shows that there are too many pans on the stove, too many meetings, too many waiting replies, too many tests, too many …

The women in this chapter all contributed by showing me ways to keep life in balance, to understand and focus on what mattered to me. In turn, they honored that what was important to me was different from what was important to them.

Superwoman Lunch

Have you ever felt pure gratitude that the Almighty in the universe saw fit to bring someone into your life? Can you point to the exact reasons that you are a better person because a certain someone is in your life? That's Dawncelie (pronounced dawn-see-lee).

Dawncelie and I struggled for one reason or another to make a connection for lunch. As she was quick to point out, "God has a plan for each of us." It became abundantly clear why our lunch didn't work until a specific week. That week, I needed her support and especially her sense of reason for a difficult decision I had made.

We met when we both worked at Starbucks Corporate in Supply Chain. During most of our careers, we were on different teams.

Sometimes our paths would cross, and we would work directly together. Dawncelie possesses many key features that a lot of my friends have—a vivacious laugh, a brilliant smile, and always dressed to the nines. It is her uncanny ability to listen and offer advice that puts her in a category all her own.

One conversation that I recall we had at work impacted me deeply. It likely started with my attempt to juggle everything. The exact beginning of our dialogue doesn't matter as much as what I recall she said at the end. "Heather, you don't need to be Superwoman."

Of course, in that fragile moment, my eyes welled up with tears. I had been trying to keep it all together, the work-life, the mom-life, the spouse-life, the friend-life—all of it.

I wasn't failing. Yet, I was not thriving. For a strong, vibrant woman whom I respected tremendously to tell me it was okay to not be perfect was freeing, and to this day, powerful.

I still hold those words in my heart like she told me ten minutes ago. I can harken to the kindness and practicality of her voice that day more often than my pride will allow me to admit. Her permission to be flawed allowed me to be the best version of myself for my kids, my husband, my friends, my employer, and most importantly, myself. That was why I was excited to connect with Dawncelie for lunch.

Our lunch was at a restaurant overlooking the waters of Puget Sound. Dawncelie walked in as she always does, as the most beautiful woman in the room. She owns the room even before she speaks.

I fought the urge to burst into tears. I needed to see her more than I realized. With her warm, embracing hug, the cracks in my foundation began to heal, fill in, and solidify. It takes an extremely special human being to do all that in a single embrace.

After our meals were served, I looked at the red plaid carpet and then out onto the waterfront. With gray skies, it was a blah day in the Pacific Northwest. "Dawncelie, I have to make a very difficult decision, and I need your advice."

She looked me directly in the eyes and said, "Lay it on me."

My voice shook as I tried to gain some confidence. I cleared my throat. "It doesn't look like there is going to be an opportunity for me to return to Starbucks now that my Coffee Break is over. I don't know what to do. Do I keep trying to find something? Force something that doesn't exist? Or do I walk away?"

She could sense my dilemma. She asked, "It's the people, right? You don't want to give up the people?"

This time, my tears gave way. "Yeah, there are so many terrific people I've worked with over the years. I hate to let that go as if I am quitting."

She waited for me to exhale. Once I did, she said, "I get it. I understand. However, at some point, you must realize there is a new path and a new adventure for you. You are meant to move on. You are not quitting on your friends and coworkers. You are quitting on trying to get a job where there is none."

She was right. I needed her words of reassurance to tell me it was going to be okay.

After we quietly put the elephant in the room to bed, we immediately fell into our familiar dialogue. Dawncelie understands what the phrase "promotional launch" truly entails. Some of our promotional efforts at Starbucks felt as complex as launching the space shuttle. We survived many promos where failure was not an option. Soon, my tears turned to laughter, recalling the moment that "Someone needed their chocolate curls on DAY ONE of HOLIDAY!"

Dawncelie is the epitome of a warrior. I used to think the word warrior was reserved only for men who were 6' or taller with a strong physique. A song phrase by Sully Erna once made me realize and understand that a warrior has nothing to do with gender or physical appearance. He sings about fighting with a warrior spirit that exists on the inside.

Dawncelie not only possesses a warrior spirit, but she has faced difficult personal challenges and has come through them. She makes me see that I, too, am a warrior. "You have a path, Heather. Know that. Trust that." Those words and actions are what make her a true leader.

We also spoke of her grandma during our lunch. Her grandma is one of my favorite topics. An equally vibrant and many times over feisty woman, Dawncelie's grandma is well into her nineties.

"Do you have any recent pictures of you and your grandma?" I asked. The pictures she shared were of a woman who sparkles from the inside out. Her grandma is a matriarch who is highly revered and deeply respected. Their relationship is strong and paramount.

Smiling, I said to her, "You know, Dawncelie, I miss my grandma when I hear the stories of the two of you together. My grandma is ninety, soon to be ninety-one. A relationship with your grandma is like no other."

She knows how fortunate she is to have her grandma here, as do I. "Heather, we are blessed to be this age and still have our grandmothers."

Dawncelie is one of the most influential women in my life. I heed her words. I absorb her advice. I do my best to reflect her example. I don't need to be Superwoman.

Role Model Lunch

There is a saying that suggests one can only truly connect with people at weddings and funerals. My lunch with Tobi happened because we reconnected during the latter—a funeral.

Several months prior, a dear co-worker from Starbucks passed away unexpectedly. Nancy's death was a shock and a wake-up call for many of us to heed signs of ailing health. She was a sweet woman with a heart of gold, who had a wonderful zest for life and respect for all around her. I can still hear her infamous "howww arrrreee ya?" in my mind.

At Nancy's Celebration of Life, many people conveyed how she embodied the spirit of carpe diem. She was spontaneous with her travel and kind with her words.

One person's memorial speech that stood out for me was Tobi's. Tobi had the privilege of being Nancy's boss at one point. She spoke with passion and conviction. It made me smile. Not because of the words she said—it was more for the memories of days gone by.

After the ceremony in the Starbucks corporate building, I took a chance and approached Tobi. With determination, I told her, "You know, I would follow you to the ends of the earth to work for you."

She laughed and appreciated the moment. "Aw, thanks, Heather." She explained, "Funny story. I tried more than once to get you to report to me, sadly to no avail. There was never the right funding, or it was never the right time. Now that I am no longer with Starbucks, who knows if it will ever happen."

What mattered in that moment is that I realized, yet again, how very fortunate I am to know the people I know. The ones who inspire me. The ones like Tobi who embody the kind of boss I would like to have.

"We should connect for lunch sometime," she emphatically suggested. I was thrilled that my Coffee Break was the perfect reason to make it become a reality.

We met for lunch at a lovely restaurant on Mercer Island called the Roanoke Inn. This quaint place looks as if it were transported from the East Coast, with its soft grayish-blue siding and contrasting white trim and dormer windows on the top of the roof. Even the white curtains in the windows gave this place an eighteenth-century charm, despite it being founded in 1914.

As we sat across from each other in our respective green booths, I quickly understood that Tobi is a kindred spirit. It all starts from our beginnings—both of us are Western Pennsylvania gals with family ties still in the area.

Our journeys separated from Western Pennsylvania. She shared an account of her time working in the recording industry. "Yeah, and one day R.L. Burnside walks into the office and …" My open mouth shut my ears from hearing the rest of her story properly.

Her wonderful adventures as an expat in Europe were enviable. "You would love the culture and lifestyle there, Heather." I am sure my mouth was gaping open then too.

The conversation bounced around, and there were many moments when we learned how much we had in common, such as our family upbringing or our shared understanding of each other, like being female in the male-dominated industry of Information Technology.

Sometimes, I felt like words didn't even need to be said between us; it was comforting to be in the presence of someone who understood me. During our lunch, Tobi was precisely the person I needed to remind me of my abilities and vision. "You get out there, Heather!"

At the time of our lunch, Tobi was between jobs. She was narrowing down her interviews with one particular company. I sat as the sun shimmered in through the windows, listening intently. Learning. Absorbing. Being grateful.

I don't know if it will ever come to pass that I work for Tobi. She is an example of whom I aspire to work for and even whom I would like to emulate should I ever become a manager. Tobi is relentless in making sure that people come first, even when it means going toe-to-toe with leadership.

She is loyal to her team and driven to succeed, yet not at the cost of others. I appreciate all of these characteristics in a manager, and they inspire me to work hard. No matter where she lands, I know Tobi will succeed, and a company will benefit tremendously.

I have a Page-A-Day calendar on my desk. Around the time of my lunch with Tobi, there were two pages I wanted to keep. One said, "If it scares you, it might be a good thing to try." The other said, "Find your inner warrior."

Tobi epitomizes both phrases with her professional goals and demonstrative leadership. She helps me to realize that life is truly meant to be lived, carpe diem. Seize the day, seize the moment, seize the opportunity. Because scary things are good to try, and I am a warrior too.

The More the Merrier Lunch

This lunch was fun because it was a reconnection, a connection, and an introduction. Previously, when Kaycee, Robin, and I tried to have lunch together, I took ill and had to cancel. I figured it would be difficult to ever get us back together.

Sometimes, that was the harsh reality of trying to have fifty-two lunches.

When an opening in my calendar became available, I reached out to Kaycee to see if she wanted to be my lunch for the week. She is the friend who always thinks of including others.

True to form, in a way that endears Kaycee to me, she said, "Well, I know that Robin and Anthony are between jobs; could we include them too?"

I was ecstatic, "Of course! I would love for us all to meet up!"

We met at a family-run Greek restaurant. The place was decorated with various-sized statues and busts, along with random, tasteful wall décor of multiple colors. Our booth seating allowed us to catch up with each other. At that point, we were all Starbucks alum. Or as we often joked, "Promoted to customer."

Our orders were easy for the server to process: four gyro salads. I can't tell you the last time I was at a restaurant where four people ordered the same lunch. For some reason, I got a kick out of that.

"I have never met you before, Anthony," Robin quipped. My mouth dropped open, and I turned a dozen shades of red! What kind of lunch hostess was I? I had assumed they knew each other.

"Oh, I'm so embarrassed," I said. "I had no idea that you two had never met before today!" After getting past that awkward phase, it was clear that it was only a matter of time before the universe put them at the same table.

Kaycee and I had fun listening to Anthony and Robin get to know each other. Although they didn't know each other personally, they did know some of the same people. As our salads were delivered and the smell of tzatziki dressing filled the air, I said how glad I was to introduce them.

What made this lunch unique was that all of us were in various stages of unemployment or time off, which allowed us the luxury of time to talk about where we've been and what we've been doing.

Even though we each had our immediate support networks, there was something about this small group that was like an extended support network. The larger group, like ours, helped validate feelings, concerns, and beliefs. There was instant support and a sense of being heard. I sat in my seat, nibbling on the last of my salad, and thought, *I believe each of us needed this lunch and safe time together more than we realized.*

"Do you remember that time at the Open Forum when Howard said ..." Kaycee is also always good at bringing us around to conversations focused on days gone by at Starbucks. Open Forums were legendary, a chance for everyone and anyone in the corporate headquarters to attend a Q&A session. Subjects and topics of the open forums varied. If a person were brave enough, they could ask a question and often receive an answer in that moment.

In addition to the Open Forums, we remembered former leaders and old moments. While people often recall slightly different memories, some of ours were the same. "Oh my goodness," I started laughing so hard, I was afraid I couldn't get the memory out, "do you remember the day of the 'reply-all' email fiasco?"

That was a classic moment when someone accidentally sent an email to the entire company, and all the recipients' names were listed in the "To" section instead of the "Bcc" (blind carbon copy) section.

Pretty soon, it became a comedy of errors when people kept hitting reply-all to stop everyone from hitting reply-all, or in one unfortunate moment, a person thought they were sending a private and direct email to scold someone: "You got that, Kevin?!"

The conversation over the course of our lunch followed the same pattern as our friendships. Kaycee is inclusive and ensures that people are valued by how she listens. Robin is steady with her friendship and support. Her strength and ability to listen are unwavering.

Finally, Anthony is always curious about learning more about a person or situation. This led to our spirited discussions and, overall, a very pleasant lunch. The energy, happiness, and general love at our table carried throughout the restaurant.

Turning to Robin and Kaycee, I said, "Can you believe the last time that we spent any kind of quality time together was for Robin's birthday in (GASP!) May 2012! What a weekend that was!"

Quietly, as if swearing him to secrecy, I turned to Anthony and said, "That weekend was complete with flames on birthday cakes and even *maybe* in a tree. We spent the weekend in the ever-beautiful Gorge area along the Columbia River. We took in the breathtaking views, the delicious food, and perhaps a glass of wine or eight."

Fast forward to today. Now we are all still living in relatively the same areas, yet it isn't easy for us to connect. It is unlikely that we will ever return to work under the same roof. We are all okay with that as we are realistic.

I thoroughly relished every second of this lunch. Each person brought beauty, spirit, care, concern, and humor to my life. With these three, I am loved, and I love each of them. In their own ways, they remind me I don't need to be a superwoman. I need to be me.

Steady Lunch

Have you ever encountered a person whose calm and steady voice instantly puts you at ease? Someone you would like to talk with all day because they are intriguing?

Not every lunch went as planned. When I picked Mary up at her home, we intended to go to a new Mexican restaurant in the area. We arrived only to find that the restaurant was closed to prepare for its grand opening. Apparently, there had only been a soft opening, and as it happened that day, they were closed.

It was kind of humorous, as we weren't even certain we wanted to go to that place. We had already heard some bad reviews regarding the service during the soft opening. Our adventures, which would have allowed us to try a new restaurant, would have to wait. Luckily, we had a reliable backup plan, a Thai restaurant near our homes.

Mary and I first met through our kids' club swim team (as opposed to high school or summer swim leagues). As I was enjoying my pad kee mao (large noodles with vegetables dish), her eyes and voice took on a happier and happier tone. She lit up when she talked about her work in career counseling and job placement.

That's Mary. She is someone who loves her profession. Without even being intentional about it, she makes me want to do something that drives my passion and happiness. "I love helping people find that right career path for themselves," she told me.

Her personal work journey has been filled with the usual ups and downs, highs and lows. I would not presume it has always been rainbows and unicorns. Hirings, layoffs, job pauses, promotions, etc. Throughout her career, she seemed to know what she wanted. Mary has the philosophy that when she has a vision, cloudy days are simply a chance to rest a little longer before the push begins again.

She set down her fork and asked, "What will it look like when you return from your Coffee Break? Will you stay in the same department? Get something different? It seems that upon the conclusion of this sabbatical, you will be knowingly throwing yourself into the world of the unknown."

I sighed, "As you know, the duration I am taking does not guarantee me any position with Starbucks. By taking an entire year off, I know this and the associated risks. I am okay with it all. I have invented, reinvented, and re-reinvented myself to find that job that makes me happy and drives my passions."

In the quiet of the restaurant, she said, "Tell me about some of your old jobs." It was my turn to light up. "What is still probably one of my favorite jobs was working for Half Price Books when I lived in Dallas, Texas. It had it all: a small family-owned environment, a bonus program for all employees, a reasonable pay scale, a good career path, and most importantly, a fantastic team—*shout out to my Saturday Morning Buying Crew!* I only worked there for two years, and yet some of my fondest working memories are during that time."

What was occurring to me during our conversation was that no matter what I choose, there will be a degree of sacrifice that happens. It comes down to how much of myself, my life, my income, my whatever I am willing to give up to gain happiness, passion, and fulfillment. That's where Mary offered a steady, listening ear that day.

Even though we met during our kids' club swim, our boys were on the same high school swim team too. Therefore, Mary and I took lunch to discuss the world I was leaving behind and the world she was inheriting, High School Boys Swim Captain's Parent.

My tiara was now resting on her capable head since her son was going to be a junior captain. I was happy to see that she would be helping to guide and lead the boys' swim team. In her calming voice, she asked me to share some of my learnings and some of the *don't worry about this, worry about that* moments.

Of course, we talked music—my favorite subject. Prince, specifically. She is one of his biggest fans. Almost giddy, I said, "I think it is important for our kids to know the music that preceded their generation, would you agree?"

She nodded that she did. "I hope our children can identify the names or songs of pertinent musicians. Their lives are simply enriched in ways they have yet to understand when they listen to music," she said.

Finally, our conversation centered on my quest to achieve fifty-two lunches. "Oh!" I exclaimed, "They have been simply wonderful! The opportunity to focus on one person (or sometimes more) for a dedicated period is an absolute gift and joy. Frankly, it is almost becoming a lost art."

Then, as if she read my mind, she asked, "Have you thought about writing a book about it?"

Thank you, Mary, for steadying my vision and inspiring me to write this memoir.

Mary delivers a sense of calm purely through her voice and demeanor. She is someone whose life emulates vision and purpose, and she makes me want the same for myself. Mary is someone who truly embodies "The Most Beautiful Girl in the World."

The Wrap-Up

My personality is not inherently calm. (Right now, I can seriously hear ALL my friends and family say, "No Shit, Sherlock.") As much as I wish that I could be calm and serene, in most, if not all, situations, I am not.

Walk into any self-help section in a bookstore, and you will see books that dispute each other: *How to Have it All!*, *Don't Give Up Your Sense of Self!*, and *How to Add More Than 24 Hours to Your*

Day. Okay, I made that last one up. If it could be written, I'm sure someone would have done it by now.

In addition to my anxious demeanor, I am also a perfectionist. (Such a great personality trait for an author—not!) I wish I knew where or when in my life I decided that the perfectionist path was best for me. I would hurry back and tell that version of myself to STOP!

There were often grouchy mornings, late nights, missed moments, and irrational reactions that I displayed while my kids were growing. Some of it was the worry that they weren't taking their educational opportunities seriously enough, or that they had too much screen time ... or ... or ...

Standing in the coffee kitchen at Starbucks, Dawncelie really grounded me (Hey, look, a pun!) into a moment that I wished I had two decades before. However, I have a sneaking suspicion she went through the same behavioral pattern and saw someone in need. She is the kind of person who will help when she knows it is needed.

Existing in this world is not always easy. In addition to Dawncelie, the other people in this chapter all found a way to help me discover the best and most effective version of myself. Notice I did not say "efficient"—that would imply that I was trying to do it all and cracked the code.

No. Each of these lunch guests taught me lessons on how to show up, either by pacing myself, being true to my vision, being inclusive, being thoughtful, or being steady.

CHAPTER 10

IT'S NICE TO EAT WITHOUT A
BUNCH OF CRAYONS ON THE TABLE

"When you quiet your mind, you can enter a world
of clarity, peace, and understanding."

–Alice Coltrane

When anyone flies on an airplane, the flight attendants perform a safety demonstration on the features and what to do in the event of an emergency. During this illustration, there is a part about the oxygen mask that will drop from the ceiling above for each person to use in the event of loss of cabin pressure.

Each time, the flight attendant pointedly verbalizes that "you should place your oxygen mask on first before assisting others." This brief sentence has become a mantra for self-care and respite. I am no good to my family if I do not take care of myself first. I will neither have the time, energy, nor the favorite corporate jargon word … the bandwidth to be the wife, parent, friend, family member, or coworker that is required.

Time and again, I have been reminded, sometimes politely and sometimes rather insistently, to "put on your oxygen mask first, Heather," either by my husband, therapists, or friends.

It is such an easy analogy to recognize and understand. As soon as I hear the word "oxygen mask," I see the opaque bag with black lettering, the thin lifeline tube connected to a source, and the ever-familiar yellow circle with the elastic straps. It's someone else who is wearing their mask, helping me put mine on.

Something beyond a one-week vacation, my Coffee Break was an opportunity to find respite and engage in self-care so I could be the parent my soon-to-be-adult children needed. They were trying to figure out their worlds; they needed a voice of reason and, most of the time, simply an ear to listen.

The lunches in this chapter were with people who sought out their versions of respite or pause. As unique individuals, we all have a different version of what works best for us.

Some people paused briefly, another had a Coffee Break like mine, and still another made a dramatic shift. I learned a great deal about taking an intermission from each of these lunch guests.

Hairy Lunch

Every five weeks, I sit in a chair and talk to the mirror. Okay, well, perhaps maybe not to the mirror itself. No, I am not the *Saturday Night Live* character Stuart Smalley.

More accurately, I talk with the other person in the mirror, my hairstylist Stephanie. I met her after my previous hairstylist started flaking out on me. She quickly became "mine." (We become oddly possessive with our hairstylists once we find a good one, don't we?)

Stephanie had a vision and a plan, which quickly ended my constant attempts at changing my hair color and/or style. No matter how much my kids begged me to change my hair color after I met her, she would veto it. The day a random stranger complimented my hair, aha! That's why I trusted Stephanie. Ever since that fateful day, I have relinquished my rights to what sits on top of my head. Stephanie owns my hair. Period.

Stephanie was exactly who I needed in my hectic life. She is calm, laid-back, and a great conversationalist. After my appointments, I realized how much better I felt on the drive home, even on the days when I was so tired that I fell asleep in the shampoo bowl. (True story!)

I moved from salon to salon with her. I swear I would go to the ends of the earth for her. Over the years, I have survived all four of her pregnancies! You think I'm kidding?! Nothing sent me into more of a panic than worrying if the substitute would do as good a job. Fortunately, they did.

Through the years, we have talked about everything under the sun and then some: kids, spouses, families, illnesses, deaths, weddings, etc. I often booked the last appointment of the day. It gave us the chance to sit and talk more after she was finished with my hair; that was a joy for me.

Stephanie's life is busy and hectic, running a business, home-schooling, and raising four very active hockey prodigies. Perhaps prodigy is a bit premature, right now. Regardless, with four squiggling, squirming, curious, and growing sons, she is a pro when it comes to knowing how to manage with grace and humor.

Finally, we could sit across from each other. Our lunch began by catching up—as we often do—on family. If I walked into her home on Thanksgiving, not only would I already know everyone's name, but I could ask Liz how her nursing studies were going, how Vic was dealing with the new shift at work, and how Michael likes the new company. Each of us has become an auxiliary family member over the years.

We talked about her boys and the newest addition, Luna, their five-month-old dog. I have always admired her sense of calm amid Legos, Hot Wheels, crayons, hockey sticks, and all the other activities. Or the glint of mischief as she talked about shenanigans that her oldest boy pulled off, hiding the second one's toy trucks. I wish I had had her patience when I was a mom of youngsters.

Calm and serenity were never my strong suits. This meal highlighted the differences in our parenting approach. Hers is pragmatic as opposed to my anxious style. As Stephanie and I sat there, I could see her relishing the moment. From her tranquil face, I could tell that she appreciated the opportunity to eat and not worry about cutting someone's food or preventing someone from spilling their drink.

She looked at a family eating their meal nearby and said flatly, "It is nice to eat without a bunch of crayons on the table." I nearly spat my unsweetened iced tea across the table. I knew she was a genius, not only for her mad skills with my dome, but also for her wisdom in that quote.

As I let her statement sink in during our lunch, I realized that I was beyond that stage with my teenage children. Yet, until that exact moment, I never recognized the rite of passage had concluded. My children stopped requiring a black and white placemat to color or play word games with a handful of primary color crayons.

While I experienced some guilt for failing to realize it had passed, I still didn't miss the days in restaurants when every fiber of my being was stressed that that would be *the day* when the meltdown happened, when the tears would flow, and the fighting or bickering would ensue.

I don't pine for days gone by when my children were three or six or nine. For me, those were all very different ages, behaviors, and attention requirements.

Generally, when eating out, each of those ages could be satiated with green, red, or blue crayons while drawing, dot-to-dot, coloring, or word search for the older kids. I never did see the slightest glimpse of a Picasso or Bobby Fischer in my brood from a restaurant placemat.

Now, here Stephanie and I were in a setting where we could focus on each other. She could appreciate the chubby-fingered toddler at a nearby table without worry that she was going to need to cut up their hamburger and feed chunks into the chomping jaws of baby teeth. We could pause, smile, and return to our conversation. This lunch was less of a goal for me than a respite for her.

As we ate, I was grateful that Stephanie talks AND listens. She remembers. She laughs with me, even at me. We tear up when a pet dies. Every five weeks, when I say "Mirror, mirror on the wall …," the reply is the one standing behind me, with a heart so true, is the fairest of them all. She is the very person who helps me see my own beauty inside and out because she is beautiful inside and out.

Oh, and she is someone who keeps my secret of how gray I really am! (Wink!)

Reflective Lunch

Not long after we moved to the Seattle area, I met Kelli and her family when we briefly attended the same church. Afterward, we continued our friendship when I began working at Starbucks, where her husband, Steve, also worked. Over the years, she became a big part of my daughter's life.

As opportunity would have it, I was able to hire Kelli to take my daughter, Bridget, to her swim practice each day. This became an important moment in my daughter's life.

Although the trip was not long, the two of them covered many topics. Kelli was able to talk with my daughter about the immediate moments that often followed a middle school day, including teachers, other students, and classes. My daughter was not a shy person, and naturally, the two of them created a wonderful bond. In Kelli, Bridget found a trusted confidant and pseudo-aunt.

Part of the fun of my fifty-two lunches was that sometimes I drove the lunch guest to the restaurant. I picked up Kelli on a wonderfully sunny day in January, a true rarity in our part of the country. Like she had done with my daughter, we chatted the entire way. There is nothing like a sunny winter day in the Pacific Northwest. It truly warms the heart and, more importantly, the soul.

The restaurant offered breakfast every day until 2 p.m. What's not to like about that?! Naturally, I ordered the crab cake Benedict. Yum! Her huevos rancheros looked equally as delicious.

After our food was delivered, Kelli asked if she could pray before we ate. This was a first for my lunches. I was humbled and honored. She knows my family and me so well and she knew this meant a lot to me. Her blessing was beautiful. With my head bowed, I was near tears as I remembered that day was also the twenty-seventh anniversary of my cousin's passing.

Our lunch equally reflected the warmth and sunshine outside. We talked about her nanny job. She cares for a few children in her home. Drawing from my experience of her caring for my daughter, it was not difficult to imagine the ones she watches now are treated with the same kindness.

Naturally, as often happens during the lunches, the subject turned to our children. Her two girls are about three to four years older than my children. Occasionally, one of her girls would also drive my daughter to swim practice. They became like older cousins in my daughter's life too. We discussed what her daughters were doing now. They are wonderful young women finding their way in this crazy world.

There is an immediate camaraderie that exists when raising daughters. Kelli and I compared notes on what it is like to raise a teenage daughter, specifically one who is creative and artistic.

As I put down my fork with a soft clank, I said, "It seems to me that creative-type children see and experience the world very differently from most others their age. This creates certain challenges and many wonderful moments."

She nodded in agreement, "I understand what you mean."

Sensing her reassurance, I continued, "Some issues in 2019 are unique to raising a child in this age of social media and instant everything. Yet many challenges are universal to any parent in any generation. Having your support to help navigate the waters is more important now than I ever realized."

As the eighties music played over the speakers, Kelli understood a lot of my observations and frustrations from working at Starbucks. My voice was perturbed at one point: "There were moments when I could not understand the vision or the goals for the year."

She nodded and smiled. "I get it. Steve says the same things too."

She has a calm, sensitive, and centering voice. Knowing someone like Kelli is a gift. Our lunch conversation helped me realize that with these lunches, *a network is critical to my well-being.*

Reflecting on my networks, I envisioned a spiderweb. Something that has tracks and critical intersection points. This easily translates into relationships I have with people I know. While some may be purely from a friendship perspective, others are on a career track with a friendship intersection.

I once heard that a spiderweb is a stronger structure than any steel bridge ever created. "Spider silk may be six times stronger than steel by weight, but it is its toughness that makes it so special, as it allows it to absorb a large amount of energy without breaking."[5]

Pondering further, this makes sense. A web captures dinner, fosters and grows a family, and provides a transportation lane. Plus, when it traps water droplets, it can create some of the most picturesque photos.

With our bellies full and the food nearly gone from our plates, I knew our network intersected at the critical point of friendship and trust. I entrusted my daughter with Kelli's care. I was overcome with thankfulness at how fortunate both my daughter and I were to have Kelli in our lives.

Driving home, I considered my own network and thought in terms of that spiderweb. Who shored up the intersection points? Who was along the tracks? Who gave and received my energy? We all balance on a spiderweb in this life together. As I parked my car in the garage, I paused, reviewed, and, like Kelli did before we ate lunch, said a prayer of gratitude.

Former Work Spouse Lunch

When you have worked at a company for any length of time, you undoubtedly begin to forge tight relationships. Depending on the situation, these relationships might become like having a work spouse. Scott was my former work spouse.

---

[5] scienceinschool.org/2007/issue4

Scott and I were on the same sourcing and supplier management team at Starbucks for about five years. Our area was high-stress because we worked on Beverage Components. The expectation was that we would hit the promotional launch dates and cost-savings expectations.

Sounds easy, right? Not for Beverage. Projects frequently ran late, and our cost savings endeavors were always met with obstacles, pushback, and generally ridiculous blockages from decision-makers. To say it was a difficult area feels like a deep understatement. Even with the daunting environment, Scott and I NEVER missed a launch date for promotional beverages.

Our Beverage Components team of four was small yet mighty, full of snarkiness and sarcasm. To combat the stress, we took to teasing each other, defending each other, supporting each other, and my favorite—Nerf gun wars.

Yes, Scott owned a pair of Nerf guns and gave me one of his. The foam projectiles created much-needed release and even laughter. We sat across from each other with targets (literally) on the backs of our chairs. Now and again, I would hear a "click click" sound followed by the familiar thwang! sound that only a Nerf gun can deliver. Once, *maybe* twice (or more!), the soft bullets would go astray, and a shoulder or arm would be the casualty. Perhaps even innocent bystanders were involved. *Perhaps.*

Scott and I spent endless hours in meetings. Endless. Hours. With the occasional "gift of time," a term that meant that a meeting ended early and ahead of the already blown hour we had budgeted.

Scott was always good at capturing "corporate speak." He had a whiteboard outside his drab tan cubicle with the various phrases worthy of a BINGO card. We would fall into fits of laughter and nearly tears, recalling meetings where phrases were dropped. NEVER under any circumstances were we to utter the corporate speak phrases in a meeting lest Scott assess a twenty-five-cent fine per word.

Scott and I worked on many complementary promotional projects. He would buy the Frappuccino® base; I would buy the toppings. From time to time, we would work with the same suppliers or back each other up. We joked with the suppliers that we were each other's work spouse.

One day, Scott and I were in a supplier meeting, talking about a project from a few years prior. Whatever the project was, we ended up finishing each other's sentences and completing each other's thoughts. I walked out of that meeting stunned. There were days I barely knew myself, and yet here I worked with someone who could answer for me—literally!

Our lunch was a great opportunity to catch up. Scott picked a rock 'n roll-themed pizza place. Of course, I showed up in my black Foo Fighters T-shirt. He was also on his own Coffee Break, which had started a month earlier than mine.

It was strange to sit across from him; it was like looking in a mirror. Gone were our worry lines and pinched faces. The lunch was not spent with darting eyes worried about someone wanting our time or thoughts.

Instead, I sat across from a friend. I said, "You know, Scott, looking at you, I see the comments I've heard from others: 'You look so refreshed! You look so happy! You look rested!'"

"Tell me about how the new business is going!" I said with a deep curiosity.

He proudly declared, "Well, I have been spending my Coffee Break helping my wife get her home healthcare business off the ground. There are pros and cons to working with my real spouse. However, by sharing a common goal, we have found that oftentimes the mundane or irritants dissipate."

With a knowing smile, I said, "I couldn't be happier for you! This is a fantastic opportunity."

We both agreed that we are living the absolute meaning of "gift of time" in our respective Coffee Breaks. We each were taking the time to be the parents, spouses, and friends that we knew were critical to our personal health and well-being. A sabbatical was truly the "Gold Standard" of what a "World-Class Organization" should offer. (How can I resist?! Yes, I owe you fifty cents, Scott.)

Scott and I hold fast to the belief that time is short and oh, so very precious. No amount of money, fame, or fortune was going to give us back the hours we missed working instead of being with family or friends. In our careers, we both sought a balance between work and life.

Without a doubt, I am extremely blessed to have Scott as my friend, teammate, and work spouse. Aside from the snark and sarcasm, he and I possessed similar values and beliefs. We each did our best to live them out every day.

Most of a person's working life is usually spent with someone other than their immediate family. In Scott, I worked with someone who complemented me to the point that he finished my sentences. When I left Sourcing for IT, he took the Nerf gun back in the work "divorce."

I still miss that gun.

No Risk It, No Biscuit Lunch

Jennifer is the epitome of style and taste. Her outfits of fitted jackets, soft creamy sweaters, and black dresses are always impeccable and complementary, with a mix of class and trend. She is the woman who carries herself with a confident knowledge that designers plan looks for her, not the other way around.

It was this fashion sense that further drew me into Jennifer's orbit. While I had known her for several years while working at Starbucks, the day I tentatively asked her about the clothing stores she frequented seemed to solidify our friendship.

I explained my struggle as a short woman to find clothing like she wore. I only found clothes designed for short old ladies, primarily polyester with elastic waistbands. These clothes were not for young corporate types. I was frustrated.

Without hesitation, she named a few stores that had a solid lineup for petite *and* younger women. Pretty soon, my wardrobe was flush with skirts from Ann Taylor's petite line, Banana

Republic's crisp button-down petite blouses, and Nordstrom's petite dresses.

Her advice resulted in clothing that was age-appropriate. Her wisdom finally gave me the styles and pieces to be more confident in supplier meetings and one-on-one discussions with leaders.

It also helped that we had several mutual friends who locked our relationship tighter. Other lunch guests in this book, like Michelle, Priscilla, and Robbie, were also friends with Jennifer. We quickly became comfortable in our friendships, meeting for lunch or happy hours.

Jennifer has a beautiful soul. It shines in the sound of her laughter, where I can't help but be surrounded by warmth. When we met for lunch on the back patio of a golf course, she had made a radical decision with her job. I was all in to hear about her strong, courageous decision to resign rather abruptly. She was fed up with her role and knew there were greener pastures out there for her.

Burnout is a very real and unfortunately common experience in today's workplace. Both Jennifer and I had been feeling discouraged and wanting more for ourselves professionally.

On that warm, sunny day beneath the green sunshade umbrella, impeccably dressed in the perfect, red-toned blouse and stylish white pants, she shared with me, "I had had enough. I wasn't moving into the roles and responsibilities I wanted for myself. Worse, I had fewer and fewer advocates as people left due to layoffs or attrition. So, I gave myself the permission to quit and find something new. It feels fantastic! I'm so relieved right now."

Even though at that point I was only a month into my Coffee Break, I said, "I completely understand what you are saying. You have been trying for so long; you are extremely capable. I get the burnout and frustration. That is why I'm taking the time off too. I'm so happy for you!"

After we got the serious conversations out of the way, we both looked out onto the tee box closest to the restaurant. "Remember the Starbucks golf tournaments we participated in?" I asked.

In that happy, good-natured laugh, she said, "Oh, you bet I do!"

As if we were seeing the exact same memory, we burst into a fit of giggles. "The tenth hole at Druid's Glen Golf Course?" I asked.

"Oh, yeah, we will never forget that one! We more than carried those guys on that hole!" she said.

Jennifer and I were golfing as a foursome with two of our male coworkers. I will refrain from naming names to protect their golfing reputations. Or should I say, goofing reputations? Regardless, each hole required that we alternate between who was the first to tee off.

We drove our carts to hole number ten. Male coworker #1 pulled their driver from their bag and approached the tee box. Carefully placing the ball on the tee, he stepped back to determine the angle and distance. Side note: There *might* have been alcohol involved in this tournament.

He lined up his golf club, feet, and head. To this day, neither Jennifer nor I know exactly what went wrong with the swing, only that we had to quickly take cover. Male coworker #1 somehow hit the ball, the ball hit the earth, and ricocheted **behind** us! It was a hilarious shot, our fits and peals of laughter destroying the quiet that is notorious on the golf course.

We eventually settled down and composed ourselves. Next was male coworker #2's turn. Same as on every other tee box shot, he pulled the driver from the golf bag, other clubs clinking around, and lined up the shot, angle, and distance.

Thwap! "Duck, Jen!" I yelled.

Again, male coworker #2 hit the *same* errant shot in the opposite direction of the fairway! Our roars of laughter could be heard echoing across other holes nearby.

How in the world did both of you hit your tee shots BEHIND us?!

Fortunately, Jennifer and I were able to compose ourselves and salvage the hole with straighter and more true shots. That tournament was the stuff of legends for all of us. Jennifer and I made a reasonable duo in those tournaments. Or maybe the better way to say it was that we made good mischief makers!

As insects filled the air with their summer trills, that day Jennifer and I spent eating lunch on a golf course allowed us to find a moment of respite and relaxation. Listening to the quiet smack of a golf ball or the gentle chug of a golf cart provided us with the understanding that we both had made bold moves like a sabbatical or a resignation.

Spoiler alert: Neither of us sought the LPGA for our subsequent careers.

The Wrap-Up

When I meditate to be present, I use visualization skills. Closing my eyes and taking a deep breath, I see two hot pink sticky notes with words written in bold Sharpie. One note says, "Here," the other says, "Now." It grounds me. If only for that short moment, the visualization helps.

The opportunity to read a book and become lost in worlds and words is my ideal way to relax. There are a few books that are among my favorites; each for a different reason, and each a good representation of respite.

The Alchemist by Paulo Coelho. I have read this book several times and gifted it numerous times. Each time I learn something new about myself. One of the more famous quotes from this book occurs on page 64: "When you want something, all the universe conspires to help you achieve it." I am forever curious about how to seek my personal treasure. *What am I here to do?*

In no way does respite or this book mean for me to sit back and wait. Quite the opposite, *The Alchemist* reminds me to seek, learn, and understand. My lunches gave me the opportunity to listen to my guests' journeys; their challenges, victories, and everything in between.

Gift from the Sea by Anne Morrow Lindbergh. I first read this book about two years ago. When I finished, I shouted to my empty house, "Why did no one ever tell me about this book before?!" It was unfathomable that I had lived these many decades without anyone putting this book in my hands and saying, "You *must* read this!"

Lindbergh and I have almost nothing in common, starting with when she wrote this book. Originally published in 1955, it was a much different life for women then. I don't even need to broach the subject of the difference in our lifestyles. Yet, somehow, Anne brought universal themes into this book that rocked me to my core.

She spoke of friendship, motherhood, and the gift of solitude. Perhaps I related to it all because the setting was my favorite location, the ocean. The various shells were her examples for color, beauty, and intrigue in her life.

My lunches allowed me to pause with some of my guests for an hour or two. In some situations, that was sufficient enough to relax and continue out into the hectic world, similar to Anne's lessons.

Running with Sherman by Christopher McDougall. Discovered and recommended by my mom's book club, bookstores should thank me for the number of times I have gifted this book! One year, I got a quantity discount!

Sherman is the luckiest being in this entire world.

McDougall's book pulled at my heartstrings, and when I thought I was drained of emotions, he helped me find more. This is not a book for runners only. (Whoa! Did I really say that?!) This book taught me about learning patience and persistence. And add a dash of humor, because … donkeys.

Even though I first read this book well after my lunches, there are parallels throughout that allowed me to reflect with gratitude on my lunches. It reminded me of my guests, who selflessly gave to improve the world around them, who spoke about vulnerable topics, and who knew how to take the right parts of life seriously.

Running with Sherman inspired Mark and me.

Fast forward to our retirement years, there might be a donkey or two in our future …

CHAPTER 11

BUY THE SHOES,
EAT THE CHOCOLATE

*"The time for action is now. It's never too late
to do something."*

−Antoine De Saint-Exupéry

During my sophomore year in college, several of us went to nearby McConnells Mill State Park to do some light hiking. Nothing too strenuous, mostly walking around on the paths to spend a fall weekend.

We came around a corner and encountered a few-story-high cliff face. The rocky surface was somewhat sheer. There, we saw some people rock climbing and rappelling.

It was intriguing to us as we had never done it before or even seen it up close. We watched a couple of people carefully pick their way up the rock as they selected footholds or fingerholds, or maybe a handhold to move toward the top, where some maple and oak trees patiently waited for their ascent.

Each climber had a counterpart on the ground who was holding a thick, colorful rope. The continuous communication between these partners impressed me. The trust between each person was evident, as if to say, "I'm going to tell you my next move and do as I say."

My friends and I were fascinated. We had no shame standing on the trail and gawking at the spectacle before us. Eventually, we heard someone loudly say, "On belay!" We witnessed the climber who had reached the top begin to push off from the rock and slide down toward the earth, essentially undoing all the hard work they had done. And yet, the person did not look the least bit sad. If anything, there was an enthusiasm and excitement in their eyes.

After standing around for about fifteen or twenty minutes, someone from the climbing group matter-of-factly said, "Do you guys want to try?"

Perhaps it was the crisp fall air, or perhaps it was the fact that we were young and immortal, because we all said "Sure!" Each of us had at least the clothes to ascend with little trouble. Perhaps our sneakers might be a small problem, but the rock face wasn't too high, so it shouldn't be that big of a deal.

When it came to my turn, I quickly realized how much trust I was putting in a stranger. I felt only exhilaration. My attention was focused solely on the person who would remain on belay on the ground.

As I wrapped the blue rope around my purple sweats, they gave me the same instructions my friends had received. Rock climbing requires at least two physical traits: a thinner frame and longer legs and arms. I had one of the two features. Unfortunately, I was not blessed with height.

There was no way I was going to let my lack of height deter me. I was getting to the top! The trust pivoted from the person on the ground to me and the rock. I had to trust that I could make the right decision at the right time and not slip, fall, or teeter.

My first step was to grab the cool surface of the rock above me. The material felt smooth on my fingers. Mimicking a crab, my hand gripped a hold. Next, I had to calculate where to put my foot to ascend toward the trees with the added pressure of a small audience of friends and strangers. It took a couple of "nope, my leg is too short" or "not quite enough ledge to land my foot" tries before I started to get an understanding of what was required next.

Slowly and cautiously, the ground and I began to distance from each other. Occasionally, I had to come back a move or two to try a different approach. I steadied my breath to focus on my right hand, left hand, right foot, and left foot scaling, not realizing that the breath was truly what was making it all possible.

The fall colors of the afternoon sky were beginning to wane as I neared the top of the rock, a smiling stranger urging me to keep going, almost there. I could hear my friends below, also encouraging me.

As I reached for the maple tree that held my line, I felt such a deep sense of accomplishment. Six hours before, I never dreamed of rock climbing. Now, here I was doing it and being proud.

Before I started the rappelling portion, I looked out and admired the view. Orange, red, and yellow leaves were all swaying as if to cheer for me. Then it was time for what was the only option: to return to my friends.

Carefully, I positioned myself as instructed, nearly at a 45-degree angle. Taking a deep breath, I pushed away from the earth. Momentarily, I was only tethered to the rope as I let my body soar into the air. It was exhilarating!

Over and over, I repeated the motion until I reached the soft soil, leaves, and moss of the earth. My legs were a little wobbly, and my face was red with excitement and exertion. The adrenaline rush began pulsing through my veins.

Since that moment, I vowed to live with a carpe diem (seize the day) mentality. For me, that means not being afraid of attempting something new, finding the adventure in making a spontaneous decision, and seeking growth in a variety of ways.

Except horror movies. Those are still a hard pass for me.

Whether it was due to a dramatic life change, natural drive, or genuine belief, my lunch guests in this chapter live their lives with a sense of carpe diem.

Adventure Lunch

"Do one thing every day that scares you." This quote by Eleanor Roosevelt always inspired me. I added my own part to her quote to say, "Big thing or little thing, as long as you grow."

In the morning prior to our lunch, my friend Priscilla and I did something adventurous and something that two claustrophobic people might never try—we floated.

The idea of floating started like many of our great ideas, over a glass of wine. As we sat in the wine bar chatting, I noticed that across the street was a business called Urban Float. "Oh!" I said, "One of the guys at work told me about this place. He said it helped him tremendously with his stress. When I was skeptical, he said that it was okay if I was claustrophobic, I didn't need to close the lid."

With a bit of hesitation, Priscilla looked at me, looked across the street at the blue LED sign, and said, "Wait! I saw a Groupon for that place. Should I get it? We could do it before our lunch."

Curious, excited, and probably a little lubricated in my decision-making, I said, "Sure! Let's do it!"

Floating is a recent health trend that promotes lowering cortisol levels and easing pain in arthritic or aching joints. In a private room, an individual has their own "pod," in which they float in approximately 1,200 pounds of Epsom salt and body-temperature water. Intended to be a sensory deprivation experience for almost an hour, floating allows a person to be completely buoyant to allow healing and relaxation.

The pod is an enclosed, yes, an enclosed capsule—very space-like. It reminded me of a long version of Mork from Ork's vessel in the late 1970s TV show *Mork and Mindy*—*Nanu Nanu!* Technically, it is much larger than Mork's egg. The idea of closing a capsule and floating in either soft lighting or total darkness scared both Priscilla and me to our core. And yet, it was a "If you do it, I'll do it" moment.

The attendant gave us a tour of the rooms. Priscilla and I both breathed a nervous sigh of relief when it was explained that closing the pod lid was optional. When an hour was up, soft jets would churn in the still water, and the LED lights would illuminate.

Our final decision was to select what kind of music we wanted to listen to from a list of fourteen options. I chose "Rainforest Sounds." As I looked at my pod, I debated briefly about the lid position and whether to have lights on or off.

In a moment of courage, I decided to close the lid and float in darkness. As I lay in the water with my earplugs protecting my ears, I thought it was funny that the option to adjust the lid and lights emboldened me.

When my float time concluded and the jets and lights came on, I expected to be in a groggy, relaxed state. I felt ahhh-mazing! I couldn't believe how invigorated I felt. I was prepared to conquer the world! The energy and a clear mind were incredible feelings.

With wet hair and rinsed skin, Priscilla and I walked over to where the entire idea was hatched. We had lunch at the wine bar where we decided to start our adventure.

Over some salads and, of course, some wine, she and I compared notes. "I can't believe how amazing my mind feels!" I exclaimed.

"So do I!" said Priscilla. "I was not sure what to expect. It wasn't this. This is great!" She continued, "Guess what, I turned the lights off and completely closed the lid! It wasn't as scary as I thought! I figured I could always open the lid if I changed my mind."

Sipping some red wine, I said, "I did too. It was not bad at all. I think I might have even fallen asleep!"

With a quieter voice, Priscilla said, "I am ready to conquer the world. There is a sense of happiness and overall well-being in my body. I didn't want to tell the attendant all of that because I knew she was going to want me to sign up for the biggest membership package available."

I laughed. "Oh, I agree. I tried to play it cool and said that I would give the membership some thought, when in truth, I want to go back tomorrow!"

After the initial excitement waned, Priscilla and I talked about my plans for my Coffee Break. "Where do you plan to travel?" she asked.

"In August, the kids and I are going to Pennsylvania for some college tours for Nolan."

She closed her eyes tightly and sucked in her breath. "This can't be happening. He can't be that age already."

"He is. It is here. I can't believe it at times myself. I am so glad I was able to take this Coffee Break. It will give me time with both Nolan and Bridget because, as you know with your boys, it won't be long before they are out of the house," I said, hoping there was more excitement in my voice than trepidation.

After our lunch, we decided to treat ourselves to raspberry cheesecake from the dessert menu. "You know, Priscilla, I am so glad we decided to have our mini adventure today. There was something in facing our claustrophobic fears and realizing it wasn't as bad as our minds led us to believe. It was empowering. It was wonderful. And honestly, it helped to have my friend along too. Cheers!"

Our glasses clinked, knowing we would go back. And knowing we would seek other adventures too.

Red Heels Lunch

As soon as I saw her walk up, I knew this was going to be a fantastic lunch. Why? Because she was dressed nearly exactly as I was. Navy blue with white polka dots and killer red heels. She was in a dress, and I wore slacks and a blouse. How could this lunch date be any better than that? Oh yeah, the gorgeous tease of a summer day—in March!

Squealing loudly and with boisterous enthusiasm, we embraced. Stepping back, we compared and admired all the different parts of our nearly matching outfits. Beaming widely, I said, "Truth be told, Michelle, I selected my outfit especially in honor of you. You often wear a striking shade of red lipstick that I absolutely adore (and envy). Your warm chestnut eyes and hair are the perfect frame for that bold statement. I love your look and wanted to be worthy of that lipstick, so my killer red heels it was!"

"Well, you know, Heather, I *love* this!" she said. "Because life is short, wear the heels, eat the cake, and dance like no one is watching. And if you are dancing, Heather, you better believe that I will join in with you!" Michelle has an energy about her that makes me want to be around her.

Michelle and I met because of our children's club swim team. Like many of my swim family relationships, she and I instantly fell into a comfortable and warm friendship, spending endless hours on bleachers to watch a thirty- or sixty-second event.

She has a beautiful honesty that can be rare to find. She is not afraid to express frustration or concern in the same way she is not afraid to express excitement and pure joy. She reminds me of me. Poker face? Nah, neither of us has one. If we played poker, I'm sure we would squirm in our seats and slyly snicker over the full house we each had in our hands.

Our March lunch took place on a warm and very sunny day in the Pacific Northwest with a record-breaking high of seventy-five degrees. The temperatures allowed us to sit outside with a beautiful view of the golf course.

After we carefully clinked our wine glasses with rosé, toasting to the beautiful day and fabulous friendship, our conversation focused on swimming, of course. "Now is the perfect time to share all that I have learned from Nolan's final years of swimming," I declared.

Her son is two years younger than my son. There is an air of a mentor/mentee relationship in our discussions. Eager to learn as much as she could, she sat forward in her chair. When I finished my monologue, she said, "Thank you for being honest and truthful to help guide me with some of the conversations with Austin. He looks up to Nolan. This will be beneficial to both of us."

As the sun shone down on the green grass of the golf course, I said, "You know, Michelle, your youngest son, Evan, is one of the sweetest people I have ever met. I love talking with him about his dog. He lights up, and his voice gets excited. Evan makes me want a dog of my own. Perhaps I am biased, but I think that dog is the luckiest dog on the planet."

She laughed that gregarious laugh that I adore. "Oh, yes! That dog is super lucky, as are we!"

In a moment of vulnerability, I asked her, "Do you and your husband, Darryl, find it difficult to live far away from your family, with them in Arizona and you here in Washington?"

She sighed wistfully, "We both want the best for each other and our children. That meant sacrificing having relatives living nearby. However, this move has been what our family unit needed. It isn't all bad. Mine and Darryl's families often visit."

Then, with a gleam in her eye, she said, "I also appreciate how moving to a new area meant making wonderful new friends."

She put it so elegantly that all I could do was nod in agreement. "Same for us. I get it."

One aspect of my lunches that I observed was how many of my lunch guests let their guard down to talk, be truthful, and share. I was honored when it happened. It made me appreciate and respect that these lunches were a beautiful human art form. In our conversations, Michelle entrusted her heart to me; it was humbling and incredible.

There was a mix of sadness and joy in the moment when our lunch ended. Sadness that the time was over, and conversely, a joy that it had happened. As Michelle walked away with the sun turning her dark chestnut hair into shimmery auburn and those red heels clicking on the parking lot, I thought, *There goes my twin, and damn, we are quite the pair!*

Even if we are only twins in spirit, I can live with that. Our friendship will continue to grow. Our *Sisterhood of the Red Heels* will thrive. Michelle is someone who complements me. She makes me see a side of myself that I adore. She is the person who reminds me that life is precious and short: wear the red heels and bright red lipstick.

Michelle reminds me to: Be bold. Be unique. Be memorable. Be kind. Be unapologetically me.

Tattoo Lunch

When I was young, somehow the number thirty-nine became my lucky number. Naturally, my week thirty-nine lunch was very appropriate because I was most fortunate the day I met Lorri. She was among my first friends after moving to the Pacific Northwest.

Her youngest son, Jordan, and my son, Nolan, are almost the same age. Their birthdays are one day apart. The two boys had fun spending numerous years coordinating birthday celebrations.

When I was driving to our lunch, I got a bit teary-eyed. The Bill Withers song, "Lean on Me," played on my radio. The timing was perfect. Lorri and I have exactly that kind of friendship. We trust that the other will always be a friend and help if there is ever a need.

Lorri was there with me during one of my most personal life events.

My first tattoo.

With equal parts fascination and support, she sat beside me through the whole process, watching as the permanent and forever red or black ink pierced into my skin. Over the buzzing sounds filling the air, she teared up listening to the story of why I determined a ladybug on my left foot was the tattoo I wanted. It was a commemoration of my late cousin who died from Hodgkin's disease. The next chapter will explain in more detail my "why."

The process was nothing like what I expected. It wasn't like hundreds of needles stabbing me; instead, it felt like someone digging into the top of my foot.

Curiously, I watched as the black outline took shape, then the dots and the head were filled in, and finally, the red was added to the wings. It was an uncomplicated design, yet deeply meaningful.

During the process, the permanence was an overwhelming feeling at times. I had to take some deep breaths to steady my nerves. I didn't need a wiggly-edged ladybug! Lorri's presence put me at ease.

Over the years, we experienced our share of ups and downs, always being there for the other person. Some were humorous, like the time I asked her to help me get my son ready because I had to rush to the mall when the store left the ink tag on his suit. Some were profound, like both of her older children's high school graduations.

What has amazed me over the years is Lorri's strength, fortitude, and dedication to her family. I have always felt like I was a part of her family, celebrating birthdays, graduations, holidays, and even the occasional, "I made pancit or lumpia, do you want to come over?" *Uhhh… yeahhhhh!!!*

Naturally, our lunch began with focusing on our children. With the smells of yellow curry in the Indian restaurant wafting in the air, I said, "Can you believe our two boys are in their last three months of high school? It's scary and exciting all at the same moment. Scary because how could time fly this quickly? And exciting because we get to witness the next chapter of their lives, adulthood."

With a sense of pride in her voice, she agreed, "It's a great feeling."

"It's hard to believe that not that long ago, Tia was watching your kids. She told me how she would spend evenings researching for scholarships. Paid off big time for her!" Lorri's daughter, Tia, was our nanny for a couple of years.

"I know! Every day, when I look at my children, I know that Tia positively reinforced some of their most promising characteristics. She was fun and strict all in the same moment, yet she set reasonable boundaries. My favorite memory was the year that she made summer 'Bucket Lists' which included hikes and ice cream destinations. She was such a great example for them."

"And even though your eldest son Alex was not as direct an influence on my kids as Tia was, he still was very much in our lives, attending the birthday parties and holiday festivities and always taking seriously the role of pseudo-big brother to Nolan and Bridget."

We caught up on her work in job placement and career improvement. Her passion was infectious. "I wake up every day happy to go to work. Excited to see what new challenges I can overcome, rise to meet, or improve," she said.

When I hear her stories about her work, I think about the ripples on a pond, how her singular drop is improving the lives of many that she can immediately see, and the ones that reach far beyond her field of vision.

We also talked about what the landscape will look like and how it will be as empty nesters. With a gleam in her soft brown eyes, she said, "I don't know about you, Heather, but I am ready to embrace this next phase in my life."

"For sure! I believe knowing that we have each other and other friends in similar situations makes it less scary and more exciting. We have taken our parental role seriously, to the point where we are ready to watch our fledglings not only flap their wings, but, more importantly, see them soar."

It was as if the colorful décor around us began to swirl and dance in the delight of our conversation. "Yes," Lorri said, "getting our baby birds to fly—and soar—gives me such tremendous joy."

In the years since our lunch, Lorri has found exciting ways to celebrate her empty nest. Each year for her summer birthday, she does something memorable like jumping out of an airplane or cruising around Puget Sound on a sailboat. She has fully embraced the next phase of her life. It is inspirational for me to witness and a great reminder to live life to the fullest.

Carpe Diem Lunch

For some people, advocating for themselves is not second nature. It can seem like a fine line between being pushy and being assertive. Even these days, being assertive can be construed as rude and offensive. If Robbie had not been an assertive self-advocate, she might not be here.

I met Robbie as I did many of my lunch guests—at Starbucks. She and I began our careers there within weeks of each other. While we were never on the same team, we both worked in procurement/sourcing for many years. Around the time I moved to IT, Robbie moved to the project management part of supply chain.

That didn't prevent us from remaining friends. We would light up when we saw each other in the halls or on the stairways. We took the time to at least say hello. More often, it was worth being late to a meeting to catch up with Robbie for even two minutes. (Hint: Take the time.)

In 2017, a mutual girlfriend came to me and told me that Robbie had breast cancer. My breath stopped. *What? Robbie?* It felt unbelievable. So unbelievable that even the doctors didn't think she had it. Her medical team did a battery of tests with negative results. She was sent home with a "come back in a year for a mammogram." (Hint: Listen to *your* body.)

This is when Robbie knew she had to become her own advocate. She insisted and persisted. There was a lump; it was hard, and something needed to be done. This is when she (and many of her friends) began to learn about a more aggressive form of breast cancer known as "triple negative." *What does that mean? How did they not know she had breast cancer?* We had so many questions. Probably more so because it was our collective way of coming to Robbie's defense. (Hint: Women are a protective lot.)

I learned that triple-negative breast cancer is a far more aggressive form and only affects 10-20% of the diagnosed population. Fortunately for Robbie, that aggression was equally met by a terrific surgical oncologist—she had a team fighting for her.

Meanwhile, her friends rallied around her, making meals, sending cards, etc. Even though I am certain there were lonely days and days riddled with fear, we were going to do our best not to let her be alone in her journey.

The chemo began, and thus, her hair left. What astounded me was that during her chemo treatments, she said, "The meal you sent was delicious." I was stunned. "What?" Yes, the form of chemo she was able to receive did not make her ill. Chalk it up to very good nausea medicines, according to Robbie. While she might not have maintained her hair, she was able to maintain some sense of normalcy in her eating.

She made videos, which became a testimonial with her beautiful bald head and signature eyeliner. I cried when I saw the eyeliner. I knew that meant she was going to be alright. I told her as much. It warmed my heart to see her fight this head-on and with some sassy makeup.

If you ever want a good read about such a person, I recommend *Why I Wore Lipstick to My Mastectomy* by Geralyn Lucas. Being sassy is as much of a fight as any other approach.

Robbie's chemo process was lengthy, then the surgery, then the radiation. There was a defined path, and Robbie was hitting all the milestones. She returned to work in a limited manner.

Eventually, she increased her hours at work. We'd have coffee from time to time, checking in with each other. One day, I noticed a Band-Aid on her chest. As I gasped, she smiled; the port was out! We both teared up a bit, knowing what that meant—her treatment was over.

When we met for lunch, she was a year into remission and it looked promising. Slowly, the doctor appointments were starting to stretch further and further between visits.

"Look at you in those sassy high heels!" Robbie exclaimed. "Of course you would wear them. I love that you rock those heels!" She had always commented on and complimented my footwear. I had to pick the perfect pair for our lunch. Strappy and black with pointy spikes that made a lot of noise when I walked on the parking lot.

Our lunch on outside tables at Starbucks Corporate was a fantastic opportunity to celebrate her remission and a big life event: our eldest children were graduating from high school. We picked up food from one of the food trucks and enjoyed a warm summer day in the city. Even the birds seemed to be celebrating.

Her daughter and my son are the same age. She asked me, "Does it seem possible that you are old enough to have a high school graduate?"

I paused for a moment. It's something I hadn't considered. "No, it doesn't seem possible."

She laughed and agreed, "Me neither."

With a mix of emotions in her voice, she said, "Did you know that I have become a sounding board for other breast cancer patients? In a corporate building of 5,000 people, it is like a small town. There is a high likelihood that someone else has breast cancer. A couple of people have reached out to me to hear my story. I'm glad I can be helpful like the women before me who also had their bouts with breast cancer. As much as it was pure hell that I went through, it is good that I can share my experience with others."

Robbie has never been one to take life for granted. Her motto is: "Wear the shoes, eat the chocolate." Our lunch was such a moment to savor. Savor life, friendship, family, and sunshine. She continued to talk of the importance of being her own advocate and how she does not hesitate to share her story. "I do not say, 'Woe is me.' More like, 'Yeah, I had it, I beat it, you can too.'"

That doesn't mean Robbie is cocky and arrogant; she knows her risks and all the chaos that comes after you begin the remission path. While the word remission sounds relaxing, it is quite the opposite.

Remission means vigilance.

Which is no problem for Robbie because she is classy, sassy, and a whole lot bad assy.

The Wrap-Up

After thirteen and a half years with Starbucks, my Coffee Break ended. As much as I tried, there was no role for me to return to. My Starbucks career ended on October 1, 2019.

I knew the risks when I started this journey. Nothing was guaranteed. I accepted this because I trusted that the next big thing would be out there for me. LinkedIn became my obsession, and I applied for different roles and jobs.

At the time, I did not have an exact title for what I wanted to do; I could only describe it. In my next role, I wanted to do something that was customer-facing and still allowed me to keep up on my technical skills.

In November 2019, I was contacted by a company's recruiter. They had a role called "Customer Success Manager" that they thought I would be perfect for. Curious, I asked for more information. As the recruiter spoke, I had to play it cool. *OMG! This is EXACTLY what I was looking for!* The serendipitous moment turned into a job offer.

A Customer Success Manager works with companies to ensure that the IT platform they purchased is working according to their expectations. Additionally, if there were enhancements, I was the "voice of the customer" to advocate to the development team.

The role was precisely what I was seeking, and it was a great fit, until the fateful day when the downturn in the IT world meant that our entire team was laid off due to restructuring. While I was disappointed, I knew that meant that something else was out there for me.

The IT world became difficult to navigate. Job postings would appear, then disappear. Same with recruiters.

Then came the day of my own carpe diem. I took the time to do some soul searching. The answer that came to me was that I was no longer passionate about IT. I was ready to walk away and start an entirely new career.

I drew inspiration from these four lunches specifically. These women taught me that it is okay to be adventurous, strike out on a bold new path, try something new, and "wear the shoes and eat the chocolate."

You are holding the results.

CHAPTER 12

IT'S A PART OF LIFE

"Don't cry because it is over, smile because it happened."

–Dr. Seuss

Death. The one topic that none of us will ever escape. In planning for this section, I knew I needed to tell my own experience with death. The death of my cousin when I was eighteen years old continues to affect me.

My cousin Michael was five years older than I was. Growing up, when we were at our grandparents' home, we were inseparable, always palling around together, playing board games, listening to music, exploring the woods near our grandparents' home, or my favorite, searching the nearby creek for crawfish.

As we grew older, we would go to teen dances together. This required a bit of an effort to find someone of the opposite sex to slow dance with, because everyone assumed he and I were a couple. We had to explain that NO! we were cousins and ewww!

The day that my mom told me that Michael had cancer is forever etched in my mind. We were standing in the kitchen. She looked at me, and, with a steady voice, said that Michael had Hodgkin's disease (lymphoma). I immediately broke down. The word cancer is always scary and upsetting to hear. That wasn't the entire reason for my tears.

Recently, I had written a report on the prevalence of Hodgkin's disease in Vietnam veterans due to the spread of Agent Orange in the thick jungles. I knew and understood this disease more than most tenth graders typically would, including the mortality rates. I was devastated.

Over the next few years, he had operations, chemotherapy, and all the typical cancer treatments in the late 1980s and early 1990s that would entail. The entire time, I prayed, I believed, I did all the religious things that a young Catholic girl would do. Bargaining. Hoping. Not even for a moment considering that he was mortal. I was in my late teens; he was in his early twenties. No one dies at those ages, or so I believed.

Michael had another surgery that was supposed to help. He had a feeling that he was not coming back from this one. Call it a sixth sense, reason—I don't know. He knew something wasn't going to go right.

Sadly, he was correct. On a cold January evening in 1992, my dear cousin, friend, and pal died. He was only twenty-three years old.

I was devastated. How could this happen? Why did this happen? I was immediately in the throes of the various grief stages. Anger, denial, bargaining, numbness.

These feelings were complicated by my rage with God. Why would God take such a young, kind, and caring man? Why would God let this happen? I did all the things! I prayed. I believed. I hoped. Why did God take away MY cousin? Why? Why? Why? My grief turned to pure anger toward whom I once believed to be benevolent, God.

I was not interested in hearing "Michael was in a better place." I was not going to bend in my anger. This happened to ME. He was my "big brother," the one who looked out for me when I was young. The one who would sing "Electric Avenue" over and over with me on the stone-encased front porch at our grandparents' home. I was angry, and this was ALL GOD'S FAULT. Period.

I stopped going to church. I was not a kind person. At the same time, I was also trying to navigate my freshman year of college with a roommate who was less than ideal. Emotional and raw were the only two reactions I could muster.

Several months later, in April, I went home to visit my parents. Sunday morning came. My mom asked me to go to church. I spewed a diatribe about why I was *not* going, why I would *never* go again. What a fraud I believed God and faith to be. It didn't matter what I did. Michael still died.

She listened and again asked me to please go with them to church. Eventually, I relented. I would go, but I was *not* going to participate. If you have ever attended church with my parents, you would know that they loved to sit very near the front. Not exactly the ideal place for a grouchy, angry eighteen-year-old. Everyone was going to see how mad I was. I slouched, frowned, and did every typical body language scenario that depicted my distaste for being there.

That day in April, it was unseasonably warm for Western Pennsylvania. The ushers propped open some of the entrance doors to let the warmth and sunshine into the church. The birds were singing, giving hints that perhaps spring was not so far away anymore.

As I sat in my less-than-respectful stance, I saw something out of the corner of my eye. Something tiny and red had carefully approached my leg. A ladybug. It crawled onto my leg and sat there for the briefest of moments. My entire body began to shake as if I were shivering. Tears spilled out of my eyes and down my cheeks.

My mom turned toward me when she felt my shaking. I could barely whisper, "Michael."

I knew then and there that the ladybug was *my sign*. The one to convey to me, "Hey, I'm okay. You might not understand why I am gone, but I am okay. And you will be too. There was a plan for me. And there is a plan for you too. It is not our duty to question it. It is our duty to trust that there is a plan for each of us."

That ladybug was right. I didn't know. I didn't understand. After all these years, I still don't know, and I still don't understand. It is not mine to question. I must trust that there was a plan for Michael that ended when he was twenty-three. And there is one that continues for me.

That wasn't the only day a ladybug has graced my life and reminded me there is a plan. When I had a difficult decision or something that was deep in my psyche, a ladybug would show up.

The morning I got married in May, a ladybug was on the wall outside the bathroom where I was going to get ready. When I was trying to decide with my husband about buying a home, yep, a ladybug showed up.

When I was in my early twenties, my uncle, who had several tattoos, impressed upon me, "If you are going to ink yourself, it has to mean something." I heeded his advice.

Then, one day, I saw his daughter, my cousin, had a ladybug tattoo on her left foot. I knew immediately that was what I wanted to do too. I called her and asked her permission to copy her idea. She chided me for even asking for permission, then immediately said that she was honored I would want to do the same.

I knew a ladybug in a visible place was what I also wanted to do. That's when I elected to have the tattoo on my left foot. My friend Lorri went with me for moral support. The tattoo is a daily reminder that there is a plan for me. There is no need to question it; I simply need to trust it is there.

Death is difficult. It affects each of us differently. Sometimes we are given the gift of saying goodbye. Sometimes we are denied this opportunity when someone dies unexpectedly. We all cope differently as well. Some move through the phases of grief. Some never get beyond anger or denial.

The two lunches in this chapter taught me valuable lessons about how to live. And about the fact that death is a part of life.

Grand Lunch

This is an example where I truly did not know if my planned "Lunch for the Week" would even happen. Not because of scheduling issues, but rather, I wasn't even sure if she would be alive.

Leading up to the lunch, my grandma had a series of falls, which included emergency brain surgery. To be honest, I thought I would be returning to Pennsylvania for a funeral, not lunch. I worried as the week of the lunch approached: would she still be alive on that Friday? I wasn't sure. I was willing to do whatever I could to see her. If it meant we shared a Jell-O or applesauce in the hospital, I was up for it.

As the oldest grandchild on my dad's side, I was incredibly blessed to be my age and still have my grandma in my life.

No need to worry. True to form, my beautifully strong Grandma was available for lunch on the anticipated Friday. We met at the assisted living facility where she lived. To say my heart was full was an understatement.

In my mind, the name Lee means "strength." I know I am not wrong in the translation. I am proud of the fact that part of my name is after my grandma. It means so much that I gave my daughter the name as well. Even at nearly ninety years old and after some very scary spills, she is still a woman of deep resolve and strength.

She was in great spirits when she saw me. She recognized me and remembered my family. I wasn't sure what to expect. The brain is an incredibly complex entity.

We chatted, and I shared what was going on in my world. She smiled a lot. Despite her sense of recall being a bit slow, she still had it. That was very heartening to me. It was not at all difficult to BE in the moment with her. I was extraordinarily grateful to listen to her talk, to hold her hand, to kiss her still soft cheeks. Don't grandmas have the softest cheeks?

She was tired, weary, and still healing. There were moments during lunch when the tables were completely turned from when I was a child. It was humbling and yet an honor to help her cut her fish from the dinner the assisted living facility prepared, or to pour her a glass of ice water.

As I helped her, I recalled reading *Tuesdays with Morrie* by Mitch Albom and how Morrie realized the ALS was returning him to the infantile state in which he began in this world. He let people take care of him with grace, humility, and gratitude. I'd like to think Grandma was doing the same. She was a fiercely independent woman, and yet she kindly let me help her. No fuss. No anger. No despair. Grace. Beauty. Humanity.

It was so hard to say goodbye after our lunch. I told her, "Hey Grandma, you have a big event coming up in November. If you promise me that you will be here for your 90th birthday celebration, I will promise to be here for it too." In her tired voice, she hugged me and said, "I'll be here."

She was! A promise fulfilled! The November festivities were a splendid afternoon. I had a terrific time reminiscing with my cousins, aunts, and uncles and meeting some of the new family additions too. Dang, they were cuties!

The highlight of the day was the moment I read the poem I wrote for Grandma's birthday. It was a tremendous honor as I am her first grandchild. Naturally, we share a special bond.

While I was writing the poem, it was important to me that I got it right. It was crucial that I properly honored Grandma and respected my unique status. I recalled my first memories of Grandma and especially her singing to me.

Because I was named for her, it was integral that my poem explained and represented why it was a great privilege to have her name.

Truth be told, I shook like a flimsy fall leaf in the wind while I read the poem aloud to my family. I cannot for the life of me tell you why I physically, almost violently, shook, yet my voice rarely wavered. The best reason I can determine is that sometimes my poems are very intimate in that I want to make sure I properly revere the recipient. Regardless, I am pleased to say it was well received.

The celebration continued when I had the wonderful opportunity to visit my grandma on her actual 90th birthday! It was again promises made, promises kept. She said she would be here, and she was.

She was elated and delighted to see my dad and me. Usually, she is expected to spend the day in the common area, but my dad and I had other plans for her. We were going to help her open her many birthday cards. Honestly? It felt like my birthday! Her delight and happiness seemed like a gift to me. I was stunned by the number of people who sent cards. The kind words, the thoughtful memories, and the chance to see my grandma smile.

She remembered and would share a story about that person. With the brain surgery far enough behind her, she still had an incredible memory. I asked if she remembered some silly songs she used to sing to me when I was a child. I got her started, and away she would go. It was a great pleasure to relive those moments with her.

Then, my grandma, in her ever frank and direct way, said, "Well, I hate to cut our party short, but it is about time they serve me lunch. I like to eat their lunches; it's a good meal for me."

I loved it! To me, that was the sign of a very healthy woman! I didn't think my family was wrong when we believed that we would celebrate her 100th birthday. We sure hoped we would.

Sadly, we did not.

Grandma lived about four and a half more years through the worst of COVID and then some. Her death was expected, and yet it hit me hard. She was lonely, tired, and missed my grandpa, who died in 2008. She was ready to leave this world, and according to the hospice team, willed herself to do so.

I thought she was immortal and would live forever. Of course, she would not.

At one point in my life, I had all four of my great-grandmothers alive and, for a long time, all four grandparents. That was an incredible gift. My grandma was the last of my grandparents to pass.

At the graveside service, my uncle requested that I read the poem I had written for her birthday. I was worried that it would need to be reworked. Imagine my surprise when I realized I only had to change one line! Everything that I wrote was relevant on the day we celebrated her ninety years of life and on the day that we celebrated her transition from this world.

To Be a Lee

- A poem by Heather Lee Cleary

Dear Grandma—My first childhood memory
Is you babysitting Brian and I—I was three.

Music is a tradition that you and I would share
You would sing, and I would dance without care.

And we are still at my first memory in my tale
Sadly, it involves blood, stitches, and me beginning
to wail.

You were prepared and knew what to do
You kept me calm, singing in that moment too.

Over the years, you kept your babysitting gig,
Grandma
I will forever have countless memories of watching
Hee-Haw.

I am here to say, believe me, it is true
Minnie Pearl can't hold a candle to you.

You were the first working Mom
I knew in my early years
I remember the pride you had toiling for Sears.

We celebrated birthdays, holidays, and dinners galore
We all know we would be late if we arrived at 5:34 p.m.!

Today, my dear family, I am here to speak of some-
thing more
Of an extraordinary present I was given on the day
I was born.

Of a gift that is absolutely priceless and precious to me.
In my first moments of life, I received the family
name, I became a Lee.

There is something so incredible about the Lee women
They are strong, courageous, their love is fiercely given.

My name represents a lineage of women who astound
Whose stories are unique and not often found.

I am born of great heritage and great wonder
Yet the Lee women's achievements will never set
the news headlines asunder.

A Lee woman is not afraid or outrageously driven
She knows how to use the Scrabble tiles she was given.

I am honored and hope I possess the spirit of the name
I believe in the heritage so deeply, I gave my daughter the same.

There are moments where I am uncertain of
who I am—of me
Then I see my name, I am reassured, I am Heather Lee.

I am here today—we all are —my dear family,
Because of this woman's strength and tenacity.

This woman, my Grandma, we celebrate today
She always has and continues still to live life her way.

Grandma, you have been my beacon and my North Star
My love runs deep and from afar.

Thank you for being a strong and beautiful woman
It is a great privilege to be the oldest of your
grandchildren.

Now, I humbly ask their permission to represent
them all when I say,
Grandma Huber, ~~we wish you a very Happy 90th Birthday!~~

Rest in Peace and Serenity in the arms of your
Heavenly Father
until we are reunited with you again one day.

Grandma taught me how to live life to its fullest, singing to me when I was a child, watching me overnight when my parents traveled, letting me stop by after school, attending my high school graduation, and making a beautiful, cross-stitched picture for my wedding and the births of her great-grandchildren. Later in life, she sent me cards, and I would visit with her when I was home.

It was in the latter part of her years that she became more vocal about telling me she loved me, even though I always knew that she did.

From time to time, I dream about my grandma. In my dreams, there is a sense of comfort and love. Then there are the days when I see something and think, "Oh, I should write to Grandma about this; she would love it."

Then I remember.

This is a part of life. She was mortal.

I love and miss her dearly.

Inspiration Lunch

My meal with Paul was with the person who was instrumental in inspiring my sabbatical, and who ultimately taught me the lesson that life is short.

After careful planning for several years, Paul quit his job in lieu of a sabbatical. In 2013, he and his wife and their two daughters (the same ages as my children) sailed on their houseboat for eighteen months around the southern part of North America, to parts of South America, across the Panama Canal, into the Caribbean, and back to their home turf of Southern California. His sabbatical was all travel, whereas mine was occasional travel.

Several months into my Coffee Break, after reading his blog about his family's sailing adventures, I texted Paul to tell him what I was doing. "Well, you *must* have me as one of your lunch guests," was the response I received back. He fully supported and loved the idea of my lunches and of writing about it too.

By the time Paul and I connected, I was officially no longer with Starbucks and had extended my lunch with a different person to include dinner, still on a weekly basis. There was no way for me to know that not returning to Starbucks would be an immeasurable gift.

I met Paul when I worked in Beverage Components Sourcing at Starbucks. He was an ingredients supplier, or perhaps at that time was trying to get his company's foot in the door. History kind of blurs itself as the years pass. Regardless, if you have ever had a peppermint mocha with chocolate curls during the holidays, that was our project.

In October 2019, Paul had some business in the Seattle area. We arranged a time to meet for dinner.

Paul and I naturally reminisced about the old days. We laughed, remembering the story of the moment when I lobbed a seemingly impossible project onto his desk.

"Baker's style chocolate curls? In a jar?" he inquired.

In his very-Paul way, he went about the exercise. "You do realize, Heather, that my company has never done anything like this." He paused. "No one has, really." I'm certain he heard my eyes roll over the phone.

Paul was an energetic individual who prided himself on educating the customer. He could explain processes, crops, growing seasons, etc. Yet, he had a unique ability to be willing to learn. Or pause to understand further. What I appreciated about Paul all those years ago was that he didn't give empty promises, nor did he say, "That can't happen."

When tasked with this unique situation, he said, "Let me start to ask questions." In my opinion, this is what makes a good salesperson. There was nothing I hated worse than empty words. It made my life hell, and I surely did not invite the company back for future business.

Paul and I started to realize that this was a situation where we were curious enough and believed that *perhaps* the ridiculous could be achieved. With effort and trust, there was a small belief that it could come to fruition. Not only that, but it could also continue to exist even to this day.

Creating those chocolate curls was the project that connected Paul and me all those years ago. We accomplished the bizarre and can laugh (now) as we retell the story. (Side note: this product still exists well past both of our tenures.)

Before our dinner was served, I assured Paul that this wasn't an interview; I left that responsibility to Dan Rather. My intention was an opportunity to have lunch or dinner with someone and simply talk.

For a good bit of the dinner, it didn't matter if we were former coworkers or old chums; we discussed four of my most favorite subjects: sports, music, wine, and whiskey. Had we added in books, we would have been chatting for two more days! This was what my lunches (or in this case, dinner) were all about—I didn't have a list of *what do you think about* questions. Instead, I let the conversations occur organically.

And what a great segue! Paul had moved into a role in the organic products industry. This brought back a lot of memories from my time in sourcing. The organic industry has radically changed since I started in Beverage Components Sourcing in 2007, including reach and availability. And yet, some components of it have not changed, like regulations.

As Paul talked, I enjoyed learning about the expansions in the industry as well as some of the challenges that still exist today. Organic food production is still a very expensive process that can be paperwork-intensive. While products from some locations aren't listed as organic, that still doesn't mean they don't practice all that is involved with organic farming.

As the evening progressed, we agreed that there was something very valuable in the opportunity to focus without distraction on another individual(s) over a meal. This wasn't nostalgia. Instead, it was more of an understanding that to connect as humans is what is necessary.

We left dinner for our respective cars, promising to keep in touch and check in periodically.

Only we didn't. We couldn't.

Time marched on. I began a new job. In September 2020, an email arrived from a mutual friend of mine and Paul's. *Heather, I hate to be the one to tell you this. Paul died unexpectedly in his sleep.*

I gasped as a chill ran down my spine. *What? No. There must be some kind of mistake.*

Sadly, there was no error. My chocolate curls co-conspirator left this earth. Left behind a wife and two daughters in their late teens.

The very person who had inspired my Coffee Break was gone.

It was a tough pill to swallow. And yet …

And yet, he demonstrated to the most severe degree why you take the time with family. Book the trips. Spend moments with loved ones. Do the hobbies that you love. Do what inspires you. Insist that you have lunch with someone. Insist they include you in their blog. Demand that the right job is out there and go after it.

Live life to its fullest because we are not guaranteed a tomorrow. We are not guaranteed our next breath. Death is very much a part of life.

Paul and, by extension, his family, validated my Coffee Break, even though I wasn't seeking validation.

And yet, here we are. Every holiday season, I am sad when I see the twisty chocolate curls sitting so prettily on top of the fluffy white whipped cream in an ad. I am sad to know a family has lost their father and husband. I am sad to know we won't ever have conversations over lunch or dinner.

The moment of grief and sadness passes. I am then filled with gratitude. Grateful for one last dinner and the time we spent talking about the important things like sports, music, wine, and family. Grateful that I unknowingly had the chance to say goodbye.

The Wrap-Up

Girl Scouts was a big part of my young life: selling cookies, earning badges, attending meetings, the oath, and songs. I began as a Brownie and moved to Girl Scouts. While we mostly had the girls from our Catholic school in our troop, we also had some from the public school.

Other than the occasional mishap in an arts and crafts task, our ten-year-old lives were mundane. All except for one girl. Unbeknownst to any of us, she had a heart condition. We knew nothing about it until a trip to a maple syrup farm. It was a cold, brisk day. The kind where your nose constantly runs because the air temp is plain mean.

We walked onto the property and saw where they were tapping the trees, innocently enjoying the crisp winter day with its bare maple trees and taps holding silver metal buckets.

The process seemed rather dull until we headed to where the maple water was being cooked down to become syrup. That rich smell filled the air and inadvertently warmed our cold hands, feet, and noses.

There was a bit of commotion as some of our troop's mothers were yelling for people to move out of the way. Two moms had crossed arms into a cradle form and were carrying Monica. She was a shade of blue I had never known humans to possess. Apparently, her heart condition prevented her body from properly getting oxygen.

The moms got her to a seat near the fire and slowly let her regain her breath, dissipating the blue from her face and lips. To a ten-year-old, this was frightening and terribly confusing. My health was perfectly fine, wasn't everyone's?

A year later, Monica would undergo a routine surgery to repair her heart and make her a "normal girl" (in her words). She was excited to go to Pittsburgh for the surgery and more excited to return home to all of us rambunctious eleven-year-olds in her Girl Scout troop.

Except she didn't.

Something went terribly wrong during the procedure, and Monica died. This possibility, while probably known to the adults, was never a fathomable outcome to me and the other Girl Scouts. She was supposed to come home. *Who was going to deliver her cookies?* This was a practical and innocent question I worried about.

As a troop, we went to her viewing at the funeral home. Her glasses were perched on her nose, her skin no longer a slight shade of blue, eyes closed, and hands neatly folded across her chest as if nestling the very heart that had betrayed her. I cried into her mom's arms, "I thought she was coming home!" It was all surreal.

And it remained so. Periodically, I believed she would show up and say, "I was hiding all this time!" Or she would surprise us during high school graduation. My memory of her was forever stuck in our youth. Young people didn't die. Old people like great-uncle Barney, who was 98, die.

This is the chapter I most dreaded writing. And yet, I know that death is a part of life. Death seems to appear in two forms: shock or expectation. There is rarely anything in between.

While all my lunches were meaningful and precious, these two strike a particular chord in my soul. I will never have the chance to see my grandma or Paul again. Gone is the chance to share a meal, a memory, or a funny story.

I have learned a valuable lesson: take the time.

CONCLUSION

Several years removed from my Coffee Break, once a quarter, I meet up for lunch with twelve of my former Starbucks Partners (coworkers). Of the twelve of us, only two still remain working at Starbucks Corporate. We have all gone our different directions professionally, yet we remain dedicated to our connection.

We have roared with laughter during our lunches. Wiped tears away with our napkins. Shaken with anger at a jolting situation. Encouraged each other that "the right job is out there." Hugged. Expressed love. Said we will keep in touch—and meant it.

When I began my Coffee Break, the challenge to have lunch with a different person each week was merely that. Something fun to try to achieve. A goal to work toward and an excuse to visit with different people.

There was no way for me to know the life lessons I would gain. The ways that people would look excited as I crossed the parking lot, the giggling that would happen when a memory bubbled to the top of the conversation, the joy in my heart from seeing an old friend.

My Coffee Break was supposed to go from July 2018 to July 2019. It was supposed to only be a year. However, returning to

Starbucks was not in the universe's plan for my life. The time off was extended until late November 2019, when I found a job with a new company.

What was never in the cards was what came mere months after my Coffee Break concluded and I began working full-time again.

COVID.

There is no way that any of us could have imagined a world in which we abruptly had to cease gatherings, physical connection, and contact. Lunches were out of the question, as were hugs and airplane rides to family reunions and graduations.

For me, it meant my husband and kids were home 24/7 for months on end. It was the transverse of my Coffee Break. They were underfoot, and they were in my and the cats' way. We found ways to exist in the unfamiliar territory, although quite by chance, with my new job, we had upgraded our internet service, which avoided a lot of issues and problems.

While my family and I were fine and surviving in our home, some people couldn't get the familiar closure of a proper funeral. Some people had to delay breast cancer treatment and surgery. Some people had to drive by for birthday celebrations. Some people ran out of toilet paper—of all things.

Life stopped. Isolation began.

Isolation.

The very situation I feared I would experience while on my Coffee Break happened, outside of my control. Outside of anyone's control.

I would sometimes read back through my blog with the deepest sense of gratitude I have ever experienced.

Slowly, the world extracted itself from the cocoon of safety. Climbing out has been as sticky as getting out of a spiderweb, bits and pieces of fear, uncertainty, and worry clinging to the side of my face, in my hair, and on my mouth. Spitting it out has not been easy for anyone.

Only a few years removed from the worst of it, society seems to have a sense of what I call the "flinch factor." The jerking back from when your uncle might give your head a knuckle rub, or the big brother who threatens to spit all over your face. Those make a person flinch and be fearful.

As I reread through the lunches and events in my life, past and present, I realized that the return to normal was difficult. And expected. While it is okay to be less than graceful in my own return, I must push past the familiar and challenge myself again.

This book needs to find its way into the ether, into the hearts of those who are still struggling with isolation, fear, or even the reassurance that the worst is behind us. The chance to smile and remember an elementary school friend or an elementary school teacher is important to experience. The chance to hold a hand when the tears well up in a friend's eyes when they say, "My mom has dementia." The chance to squeal with joy in the arms of a cousin when finding out that her daughter was accepted to her dream college.

I admit that what I don't do easily since my Coffee Break is take the chance to make a new friend or suggest lunch with an acquaintance. That is where I need to rebuild from the pause of

COVID, where I need to reconstruct my life. I need to get out into society again, too.

In an episode of the *Diary of a CEO Podcast*, a guest talked about the importance of weak ties.[6] The micro moments of connection that are the foundation of friendship. Her take was that earbuds are preventing us from the simple connection of recognition, such as "Hey, don't I know you from the gym?" when you see someone in the grocery store.

The challenge I would put out to you, the reader: *How might you begin your own lunch (or dinner) cadence?* Weekly lunches are nearly impossible, which I understand. What is possible is monthly or even quarterly challenges.

Why should you do this?

I promise you, there are many lessons to be learned from expanding your world—again.

What did I learn?

I learned ...

> ... that I have friends who are dreamers and push into the unknown because that is the only way they see a future.
>
> ... that I worked with some tremendous people. That my life is far better for having met them,

[6] Steven Bartlett. Interview with Vanessa Van Edwards. December 8, 2024. *Diary of a CEO*. "The Body Language Expert: Stop Using This, It's What's Making People Dislike You, So Are These Subtle Mistakes! Your Resting Face Matters & How to Fix It!" Podcast, 2:18:28.

worked with them, and allowed them to challenge my professional growth.

… that I love running, runners, and personal bests. And that I'm not alone in this opinion.

… that travel is a beautiful way to grow my spirit, as it grew the spirits of my friends.

… that while I might have quit swimming at the beginning of practice in high school, swimming gave me some of the best friends I have ever had.

… that friends grow and change, and it is okay. Sometimes we grow apart. Sometimes we grow closer.

… that teachers, coaches, and mentors are an extraordinary bunch of humans. Thank you.

… that family is the group that holds some of my dearest memories.

… that I can be me, not superwoman. I can surround myself with others who believe the same.

… that respite is critical to continuing in a healthy way in this world.

… that life is short, seize the day.

… that death is a part of life. It's okay to mourn my loss; it is more important to revere their time on this earth.

… that a meal can be simple or extravagant. It doesn't really matter. What matters is who is across the table from me.

I learned all of this … What will you learn?

ACKNOWLEDGMENTS

The tiny seed for this book idea was first planted in my mind by my friend Mary. During our lunch, she rather pointedly said, "Have you thought about turning these lunches into a book?"

The idea was further germinated over a lovely brunch with close family friends Kirk and Mary Jeanne, the writer and the reader, respectively. I still recall Mary Jeanne looking across the table directly into my soul and saying, "Heather, you need to write your memoir about your lunches."

Perhaps it was the fuel of the delicious food or the dear company; regardless, I was energized and ready to put words to paper. I appreciate all of you collectively helping to sow the seeds of storytelling.

Of course, none of this would be possible without my parents, Jerry and Susie, bringing me into this world. I appreciate all the sacrifices and effort it took to raise me. Some days were not easy; thank you for your patience and love.

When given the role of godparents, mine were more than up for the responsibility. Thank you to Jim and Pat for being in my life from day one, too. Your love and guidance have meant a great deal.

Life with my brother, Brian, is colorful, interesting, and full of sibling rivalries. *Sorry about your front tooth.* It has been great fun being a sister-in-law to Cindy and Crazy Aunt Heather to my nephew and niece.

I was born into a large family with scads of aunts, uncles, and cousins. I am grateful for all that they taught me. A special thank you to Alena for introducing me to Shanda and Transcendent Publishing!

Along my educational journey, I had some incredible teachers and professors. For the ones who edited my English papers and critiqued my writing, thank you. See, I didn't end that sentence with a preposition!

I am forever grateful to all the librarians who have been in my life. Your dedication to books is commendable! From my earliest memories of running to the children's section, or picking up a young adult book, to taking my children to Story Time, and now, to scoring a Ready Reads book at my local King County Library, you have enabled a lifelong fan of reading. Thank you!

The tremendous Coffee Break program at Starbucks Coffee Company was a life-changing benefit. I did my very best to live up to what a sabbatical should be. I hope that other companies will follow their lead.

My gratitude to Ian, my personal trainer, for not only guiding my workouts, but also listening to me whine and complain about where I was with my writing! It wasn't all bad; there were often days when he enjoyed hearing about my accomplishments as well.

Shout out to my reading and writing pal, Joe L. Your feedback, suggestions, and overall good wisdom when it comes to books, writing, and music are all much appreciated.

To the authors and poets in PennWriters, thank you! A special acknowledgment to Terry Friedman and the writers in Area 7. I deeply appreciate your candid feedback and patience with my process.

To my "Biatches"—thank you, ladies, for your love and support.

To my wine pals, Val and Darin, your friendship has been a blessing to Mark and me. We look forward to more games of pool and shared glasses of wine!

Speaking of wine, writing can be a lonely endeavor. Thank you to UPS and FedEx for requiring my signature for wine shipments. This enabled me to have the briefest of conversations with my two favorite drivers. Chatting to hear how their days were going or how their families were doing always made my day.

My deepest gratitude to Dr. Beth, Dr. Aishwarya, Chelsea, Nikki, and Chandra for keeping my ship righted even through the most difficult of seas.

This book was not composed in a dark closet. I am very much grateful for all the guidance, wisdom, and "maybe try it this way" from my writing coach, Shanda Trofe. You are who I needed to get me across the finish line!

Thank you to Mary Rembert for your editing. I deeply believe that no book can ever be completed without a second, unbiased set of eyes.

To Peach, Joe, Scott, and the rest of my in-laws, thank you for welcoming me into the family all those years ago. I am quite fortunate.

To Kelly, Thomas, and their girls—I finally did it! Thank you for believing in me.

To all my lunch guests mentioned here or on my website, my deepest gratitude for our time together, your trust in me, and the opportunity to give you your flowers. You are each tremendous human beings! I cherished each second.

To Nolan and Bridget, I have loved every moment of being your mom. From the first time I touched your slippery skin to now seeing the fine adults you have become, I am forever grateful the universe saw to it that you were to be my children. In your significant others, Meg and Josh, respectively, I see your love grow and continue. They are wonderful humans too, and I am grateful for all that I get to be to them as well.

To Mark, my best friend and true love. I am grateful I was bold when it counted the most. You accepted me for me from day one. You showed me love. You have been every bit the father I suspected you would be. You dreamt with me, made scary decisions with me, and helped me see that I am so much more than I give myself credit for being. You always believe in me. From me saying, "Hey, I was thinking about taking my Coffee Break ..." to supporting me to see this book to completion— thank you.

ABOUT THE AUTHOR

When she isn't dashing to the front door to sign for a wine shipment, Heather can often be found listening to various genres of music, reading about musicians, or watching documentaries about music. Or reading something … always reading something.

She and her husband, Mark, have lived in the Pacific Northwest for almost twenty years and have been married for almost thirty! They are the proud parents of their now adult children, Nolan and Bridget. For Heather, it has been a joy to see them grow into compassionate human beings.

While her two cats, Cora and Callie, let Heather think she runs the household, they know better.

Every day, Heather does her best to live out her mantra … *Run. Write. Dream. BE.*

For more information, feel free to check out Heather's website:

heatherlcleary.com